CultureShock!
A Survival Guide to Customs and Etiquette

United Arab Emirates

Gina Crocetti Benesh

Marshall Cavendish Editions

This edition published in 2008 by:
Marshall Cavendish Corporation
99 White Plains Road
Tarrytown, NY 10591-9001
www.marshallcavendish.us

Other Marshall Cavendish Offices:
Marshall Cavendish International (Asia) Private Limited. 1 New Industrial Road, Singapore 536196 ■ Marshall Cavendish Ltd. 5th Floor, 32–38 Saffron Hill, London EC1N 8FH, UK ■ Marshall Cavendish International (Thailand) Co Ltd. 253 Asoke, 12th Flr, Sukhumvit 21 Road, Klongtoey Nua, Wattana, Bangkok 10110, Thailand ■ Marshall Cavendish (Malaysia) Sdn Bhd, Times Subang, Lot 46, Subang Hi-Tech Industrial Park, Batu Tiga, 40000 Shah Alam, Selangor Darul Ehsan, Malaysia

Marshall Cavendish is a trademark of Times Publishing Limited

ISBN 10: 0-7614-5510-8
ISBN 13: 978-0-7614-5510-3

Please contact the publisher for the Library of Congress catalog number

Printed in China by Everbest Printing Co Ltd

Photo Credits:
All black and white photos from the author except pages vi, 60, 138, 158 (Getty Images). Colour photos from Getty Images pages d–e, f, i, l–m, n–o, p; Photolibrary pages a, b–c, d–e, h, i, j–k ■ Cover photo: Getty Images.

All illustrations by TRIGG

ABOUT THE SERIES

Culture shock is a state of disorientation that can come over anyone who has been thrust into unknown surroundings, away from one's comfort zone. *CultureShock!* is a series of trusted and reputed guides which has, for decades, been helping expatriates and long-term visitors to cushion the impact of culture shock whenever they move to a new country.

Written by people who have lived in the country and experienced culture shock themselves, the authors share all the information necessary for anyone to cope with these feelings of disorientation more effectively. The guides are written in a style that is easy to read and covers a range of topics that will arm readers with enough advice, hints and tips to make their lives as normal as possible again.

Each book is structured in the same manner. It begins with the first impressions that visitors will have of that city or country. To understand a culture, one must first understand the people—where they came from, who they are, the values and traditions they live by, as well as their customs and etiquette. This is covered in the first half of the book.

Then on with the practical aspects—how to settle in with the greatest of ease. Authors walk readers through topics such as how to find accommodation, get the utilities and telecommunications up and running, enrol the children in school and keep in the pink of health. But that's not all. Once the essentials are out of the way, venture out and try the food, enjoy more of the culture and travel to other areas. Then be immersed in the language of the country before discovering more about the business side of things.

To round off, snippets of basic information are offered before readers are 'tested' on customs and etiquette of the country. Useful words and phrases, a comprehensive resource guide and list of books for further research are also included for easy reference.

CONTENTS

INTRODUCTION

On my latest trip to the United Arab Emirates I was equally amazed by the things that had changed as I was by the things that had not. While this book needed an update, culture is slow to change and my visit confirmed that I got it right the first time. The cultural traditions of the UAE are rooted in Islam and similar to those of the wider Arab world. Tribal identities remain strong, despite urbanisation, and the family is still the strongest and most cohesive social unit. The culture and society of the UAE are a blend of traditional and modern elements. The religion of Islam and the heritage of a traditional, tribal society form the basis of a stable and essentially conservative social structure. There is, however, a decidedly tolerant and cosmopolitan atmosphere that gives resident non-Emiratis opportunities to enjoy their own cultural and religious practices.

Despite having been gone from the UAE more than a decade, the meagre Arabic I had once known quickly came back to me upon my return. People appreciated my language skills more than ever simply because so few visitors attempt Arabic. The bare essentials: 'Hello, how are you, fine?', 'Thank you' and 'Welcome' are not hard to learn. The instant smiles and openness warmed me as nothing else could. I realise how fortunate I was to have lived in the UAE in earlier years since access to the Emiratis, to their culture, to their families and to their friendship is less available to most visitors than ever before. I cannot encourage the visitor enough to learn a little Arabic, small effort will reap big rewards.

Traditional Arabic coffee pot and jars used in the United Arab Emirates.

ACKNOWLEDGEMENTS

Once again on my latest visit, those who were willing to talk to me asked not to be named in print. I am honoured they entrusted me with their knowledge and stories. In the early 1990s my neighbour and colleague Sheri Decker lived many of the experiences with me with insight and humour. She was my touchstone, my rock and my anchor.

Christine E. Henderson was kind enough to accompany me to the UAE this time and enabled me to experience the country as though it was my first time. Bob Woods was another rare find this time around. He recently returned from more than a decade living in the UAE and was an invaluable expert source. I am indebted to them both.

I would especially like to thank Maitha for her persistence in asking an observer to participate. It made all the difference.

DEDICATION

To the Emirati people with deep admiration.

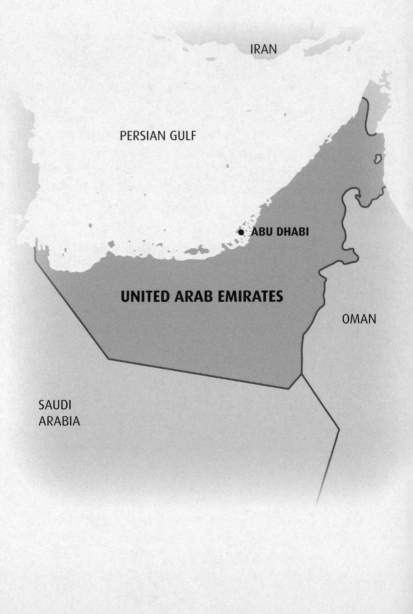

MAP OF THE UNITED ARAB EMIRATES

IRAN

PERSIAN GULF

● **ABU DHABI**

UNITED ARAB EMIRATES

OMAN

SAUDI
ARABIA

FIRST IMPRESSIONS

CHAPTER 1

'A sense of humor is the pole that adds balance
to our steps as we walk the tightrope of life.'
—Arabic proverb

THE UNITED ARAB EMIRATES (UAE) IS ONE OF THE FASTEST growing places on earth. It is a financial, political and economic success story in a region torn by conflict—an oasis, if you will, in the turbulent Middle East. In just a few decades the country has gone from nothing more than a sand spit to a destination for international business and tourism. No matter how much you read or how many pictures you see, you still may not be prepared for the energy of what is essentially a modern day gold rush with everything in overdrive.

Cranes and construction sites are a common sight in the cities of the UAE.

The cities are a physical manifestation of oil wealth converted into concrete, glass and steel that is changing the geography of the country. Skyscrapers rise out of the sand and man-made islands erupt from the sea. Of the two main cities, Dubai and Abu Dhabi, a vast majority of visitors arrive in Dubai via Emirates Air into the midst of what has been called the largest construction site on earth, where half a million labourers work 12 hours a day on US$ 3.5 billion worth of construction projects. Guest workers and tourists from all over the world abound, rushing here and there in the pursuit of money and the enjoyment of fine dining, sparkling beaches and a bustling nightlife. Every so often the cityscape is dotted with a couple of Emiratis, the men in white *dishdashs* and the women in black *abayas*. In fact, the infrequency with which one encounters an Emirati is a grave disappointment to many visitors seeking an 'authentic' experience. Almost everyone wears the dress native to their own country, giving Disneyland's popular attraction 'It's A Small World' a real home on earth.

Everywhere you go there is construction. 'Build it and they will come' has been a prevailing theme since the early 1990s and with every new construction surge, people do come. The pace and magnitude of the current construction surge is filling demand but some believe the rush also has the feel of a speculative bubble that could easily burst. Take a deep breath and relax—this is just another bigger surge funded by very deep, diversified pockets.

No visitor will escape the traffic ramifications of the development surge. The government is pouring huge amounts of money into new roads, tunnels, bridges and a metro system extensive enough to eventually stretch across several countries. The speed of development over the past three decades also has social and political consequences. In trying to construct a new and instantly modern society, the

Multinational Corporations

The UAE is a strategic jumping-off point for businesses with an international presence that wish to access the 3.5 billion people in Asia and the Middle East. This is known to the likes of LG, Starbucks, Google, Harvard and many other companies with familiar household names.

Emiratis promote gender equality, with the recruitment and advancement of women being a priority. This is a significant change from many conservative Muslim cultures; yet it is more in keeping with Islam than restrictive practices are. As a result, you will see Emirati women in public and while they are almost never alone, they may be in the company of other women rather than a male escort.

Religious tolerance is the norm and churches mix with mosques. Sites such as bikinis are common on the beaches frequented primarily by foreigners. International uproar over some Emirati cultural practices has changed some things that are seen by the West as barbaric. For example, instead of young boys on the backs of camels, the Emiratis now use robots. This still enables owners to chase their camels around race tracks in SUVs and broadcast their encouragement directly to the camel over their walkie-talkies.

The country is wrestling with prostitution—about 10,000 women from Africa, Eastern Europe and Asia are estimated to be trafficked into the UAE, as are drugs. Illegal immigration is also an ongoing frustration for the government. All these issues are reported on in the local papers in an increasingly open manner.

An uproar coming from outside the Emirati population, both internal and external to the country, is the treatment of the labourers. Disgruntled for years because of their horrible living and working conditions, they are beginning to strike and the UAE continues to be downgraded by Amnesty International for the continued exploitation of this population. The treatment of this group is not only inhumane, but also poses a breeding ground for terrorists to exploit the workers' anger. Cheap labour has built the country and is hard to give up. However, the voices of opposition may be becoming loud enough for real change to finally be implemented and enforced. The operative word being 'may'. The UAE is not a democracy and political dissent is not expressed freely though most visitors are swathed in a feeling of freedom. While freedom of expression is tolerated, it is not guaranteed—particularly not if it concerns politics. *Culture Shock! United Arab Emirates* is intended to give you deep insight into the culture and country so that you may navigate your way safely while enjoying the richest experience possible.

LAND AND HISTORY OF THE UAE

CHAPTER 2

'You have to know the past to understand the future.'
—Sheikh Zayed

CHANGE

To talk about the UAE is to talk about change. Overnight, the country has gone from a scarcely populated and little known desert to an international business and vacation destination. For centuries the Emiratis lived as fishermen, pearl divers and Bedouins, with family name and tradition passing endlessly, and little change from one generation to the next. The discovery of oil brought incredible wealth and new occupations to the small population. It has also brought about contact with the modern world and large numbers of diverse people. The country is now in a mad dash to catch up with and surpass, in development, other major cities in the world.

The country boasts comfortable seven-star hotels sporting every amenity, private beaches and shopping options that are limited only by the amount of money a tourist has to spend. Golf, water sports, camping—whatever you can dream of is available. This is delightfully surprising to visitors planning a week-long stay. Even the longer term sojourners will be pleased to find so many things to do and so many people similar to them in background, culture, and interests.

The Emiratis are working hard to adapt their culture to their quickly modernising society. They have travelled centuries in the last five to six decades. Charming and hospitable, they are spanning a long bridge of time and are doing so on their own terms. Accepting and respecting the Emiratis' terms and the sometimes surprising contradictions will help enrich one's cultural experience. It is to those who wish to look beneath the surface appearances, to meet the people, and to understand the 'whys' that this book is aimed.

LOCATION

The country is located on the Persian Gulf across from Iran. Its bordering neighbours are Oman to the south, Saudi Arabia to the north and northwest, and Qatar to the west. The entire country is 83,600 sq km (32,300 sq miles), about the size of Austria. It is made up of seven territories called emirates. The capital city of each emirate follows the name of the emirate itself. The country has 1,000 km (620 miles) of coastline on the Persian Gulf and 130 km (81 miles) of coastline on the Gulf of Oman. The UAE is building more coastline through reclaimed land, and available waterfront statistics are liable to grow.

Most of the country's land is barren desert. There are huge rolling sand dunes along the Saudi Arabian border and low, hard-packed foothills on the Oman border. Also present are a few oases (fertile spots with enough water to make some agriculture possible)—two large ones in Buraimi and Al-Ain, along the Oman border, and a string of small ones in Liwa. Salt flats are found along the coasts.

Build It And They Will Come

Many look at the non-stop building taking place in the UAE and wonder where all the people to fill the space are. In the early 1990s we wondered the same thing about the empty four-lane highways, apartment buildings and parking lots. A decade and a half has passed and this infrastructure is now bursting at the seams. The Emiratis are aware of the burgeoning Asian population all around them, estimated to be at 3.5 billion people, and they are preparing for the next wave of the worker, business owner and tourist. Preparations and efforts to attract them include improvements in governing; a freer, more inclusive society; better education and health care; and fair and competitive economic markets, to name a few. Day to day progress may seem slow, but development is going at a dizzying speed throughout the country.

The Seven Emirates

In the past, each family belonged to one of seven tribes. Each tribe was ruled by a Sheikh who administered justice. Rivalry among the tribes kept territorial boundaries shifting, and some boundaries are still not clear today. Boundaries still under dispute are marked with dotted lines on maps. While the Sheikh was the lawful ruler and leader, the *mutawa* was the community's religious leader. He led the people in reciting the Holy Qur'an (Quran or Koran) and it was through this medium that literacy was gained. Life for the Emiratis was difficult, steeped in thousand-year-old traditions and such luxuries as formal education were barely even concepts. The country and the people remained entirely unexposed to a developing world until the middle of the 20th century.

Today, the UAE is a federation of seven Arab states or emirates. Each emirate is named after its main town or city and is controlled politically and economically by its Sheikh.

Abu Dhabi

Abu Dhabi is the capital of the UAE and serves as the financial, transportation and communications centre. It has a significant port and houses most of the federal government ministries. Abu Dhabi's coast is lined with salt flats called

Sabkha. Large sand dunes of the Empty Quarter are to the south, a mountain called Jebel Hafeet is inland towering 1180 m above sea level over Al-Ain in the east, and there are more than 200 islands off the coastline.

40 per cent of the country's population live in the emirate of Abu Dhabi and most of these are in the city proper with a population nearing two million. The emirate covers a 71,000-sq km (27,400-sq mile) area and is more conservative than its popular and internationally known neighbour, Dubai. Still, Abu Dhabi has experienced explosive growth under HH Sheikh Khalifa bin Zayed Al Nahyan who was elected President of the United Arab Emirates on 3 November 2004, succeeding his father, the late and beloved HH Sheikh Zayed bin Sultan Al Nahyan.

Sheikh Khalifa is overseeing two significant changes in government, the first being improvements to efficiency and cost of public services; and second being the opening up of the economy to facilitate private investment, and for public-private partnerships to be established. With improvements in education and growth in the private sector, the government intends to concentrate on core areas of government letting political, religious and other civil society institutions take the lead for their areas of responsibility.

Abu Dhabi's wealth comes largely from oil. While trying to diversify its economic sectors, this one sector comprises 70 per cent of total GDP. Abu Dhabi is estimated to own more than 90 per cent of the UAE's oil and natural gas resources, and these resources account for 9.6 per cent of the world's total oil reserves, ranking the UAE in fifth for total oil reserves. They are currently the tenth largest oil producer, pumping 2.8 million barrels of oil per day, but plans are in place to increase production capacity to 3.5 million barrels per day. The tourism sector has risen to 3 per

President Sheikh Khalifa has a few challenges. One of these is a very wealthy native population who have been given too much without having to work for it, and thus do not value work in general, and vocational work in particular. He is sending the message to the Emiratis that they need to take greater responsibility for these roles. The other significant challenge is that the late Sheikh Zayed had many offspring who now run different segments of the government, making governing a tricky business for him.

The Abu Dhabi Palace Hotel.

cent of GDP with 1.2 million visitors arriving in 2006. The goal is to nearly triple the number of visitors by the year 2015, and thus Abu Dhabi is on a building spree, adding 17,000 more rooms to the current inventory, upgrading its airport to handle 50 million passengers, creating two new ports and industrial zones, and embarking on a grand-scale international marketing campaign at a cost of about US$ 1 billion. The key component to attracting visitors will be Saadiyat Island, a 27-sq km natural island off the coast of Abu Dhabi which will have 29 hotels, including at least one of which will be seven-star quality; as well as the world's largest Guggenheim Museum of Modern Art, dubbed the eighth wonder of the world. Completion of this Guggenheim is slated for 2020, still plenty of time to plan and prepare for 6–10 million visitors a year.

Ajman

Ajman covers 260 sq km (100 sq miles) and is the smallest of the federation of emirates. Located on the western coast of the UAE, its close proximity to Sharjah and Dubai attracts those wishing to be slightly removed from the core of these two boomtowns. Like its neighbours to the south, Ajman established its main city on a creek. It has 36 km (22 miles) of coastline and two mountain villages inland. Ajman has worked to expand its industry and agriculture but is still dependent on aid, primarily from Abu Dhabi. The emirate is pursuing tourism with a large hotel and residential complex, as well as promoting its natural assets and opportunities such as dune driving, camel riding and sand skiing.

Dubai

Dubai has become the commercial capital of the UAE. In the 1970s Dubai modernised its deepwater port, constructed a supertanker dock and now has the principal port facilities of the UAE. It has further built its national carrier, Emirates Air, into an award-winning airline, and has sought to develop itself into a regional centre and international corporate headquarters for computer and media companies. Little wonder that it is the major trading centre of the entire Persian Gulf. The emirate of Dubai covers just 3,890 sq km (1,500 sq miles) with its population concentrated in its capital city, Dubai. Population growth in Dubai has long outpaced that of the other emirates and now stands at 1.5 million, or 31 per cent of the total population of the country.

When planning a trip to the UAE, people may ask you where the country is. Just say Dubai and they will probably know the location. This is because HH Sheikh Mohammed bin Rashid Al Maktoum, Vice-President and Prime Minister of the UAE, and Ruler of Dubai is solely in charge without siblings in positions to be appeased, to slow him down or to throw curve balls at him. He can really get things done. It helps that Sheikh Mohammed is also very smart. Ask people on the street what they think of Sheikh Mohammed and the one thing they will repeatedly and consistently tell you is that he is a smart man. Dubai is steaming full speed ahead economically and as it does so, it is paying attention to every level of society, improving living conditions for all. Society has become so free and open that even construction workers, who are at the very bottom of the economic ladder, have actually gone on strike. The government is still 'studying' their working conditions, but has quickly implemented some measures to alleviate their suffering, such as making it mandatory for employers to place the entire salary of the construction worker in his bank account, thus preventing the employer from making deductions for bringing the worker over or housing him. Limits have also been placed on working hours, so work is illegal during the hottest hours of the day, during when workers have in the past died from the conditions. Time will tell if these measures are enforced.

In 2006, Dubai had well over six million tourists visit and stay in one of more than 415 hotels and hotel apartments available. They visited the world-famous man-made offshore developments along the coast, called The Palms and The World, the giant shopping centres, and played in the theme parks. Dubai's Department of Tourism and Commerce Marketing (DTCM) has 14 offices in foreign countries mounting regular advertising campaigns. We are only seeing the tip of the iceberg of what is to come.

> Visitors have arrived predominantly by air, but they will soon also be able to come by sea as Dubai, having a viable turnaround port, becomes the cruise line destination when winter strikes the Mediterranean, North America, North Europe and the Baltic.

Of note, two of the six million tourists who came in 2006 were from other Arab nations. Many of these come from politically and economically unstable nations, needing a place to park their money, and Dubai and the rest of the country can accommodate their needs, from allowing freehold ownership to providing a new stock market.

Dubai was once a single shopping city with areas dedicated to different products. There was a street or *souk* for gold, another for furniture and still another for carpets. Now all of these are consolidated into one mall after another. The city is organised into developments such as the Palm Jumeirah, Old Town, Deira and Business Bay. Its infrastructure includes service and recreation facilities, and creates micro communities. Some parts of town have managed to preserve their charm by focusing on what historically made them special, including Festival City and Palm Deira, which act as anchors and attract many people. Other areas are suffering with less in the way of retail offerings and middle to lower income earners. One of these is Bur Dubai, which traditionally housed banks and embassies. This is where the visitor would find an excellent museum showcasing traditional Bedouin life and the gold *souk*. What the visitor would not find though is parking space. Regeneration may happen quickly in this area of town as part of the Emiratis' efforts to preserve their proud traditions.

Fujairah

Fujairah is separated from the other emirates by the northern part of the Hajar mountains of Oman. Fujairah covers 1,170 sq km (452 sq miles) and is the only emirate located on the eastern side of the UAE along the Arabian Gulf. Fujairah's population is holding steady at about 140,000. Its principal industries are agriculture, fishing and boat-building, and it has virtually no oil. Fujairah has a port set up primarily as a holding station for sheep and cattle for the entire Arabian Peninsula.

Fujairah continues to build new hotels, and offers beaches, water sports and deep-sea fishing. It attracts a quarter of a million visitors each year, many of them from within the UAE. It is expanding its airport to attract more charter airplanes. Fujairah's location between mountains and the ocean offers adventure and solitude not available in the other emirates. New developments are focused in the north between Bidiya and Dibba, with work having begun on health spas, a 1,000-room luxury villa, a five-star hotel and a shopping complex. Fujairah will likely market itself as the

The Fujairah port as seen from a distance.

country's health retreat haven. Universities from the other emirates have also been relocated here to educate the locals and incorporate them into the workforce.

Ras Al-Khaimah

Ras Al-Khaimah is the northernmost emirate and covers a 4,900-sq km (700-sq mile) area. It has a population of about 250,000. Ras al-Khaimah has a rugged mountain border with Oman, several islands and approximately 60 km (37 miles) of coastline. Ras Al-Khaimah has embraced tourism and has put in place a tourism master plan which includes luxury hotels, the redevelopment of its creek, development of the Jebel Jais Mountain Resort, a climbing and abseiling (rappelling) centre, an international airport, and a free trade zone. It recently began an ambitious phase of development by investing in its infrastructure.

Ras Al-Khaimah was the second emirate to allow foreign ownership in areas designated as freehold and it was the first to pass laws to protect the foreign investor. It is only a 40-minute drive north from the Dubai area, and has become an attractive investment choice.

With its fertile soil, Ras Al-Khaimah is one of the more agriculturally productive emirates in the UAE. It is close to the Hajar Mountains, the Musandam Peninsula and the UAE's east coast, making it an ideal base from which to explore the natural beauty of the northern emirates. Tourists there can enjoy hiking, camping, snorkelling, scuba diving, sailing, picnicking and four-wheel-driving in the desert.

Sharjah

Sharjah is connected by a sophisticated network of highways to Dubai and Ras Al-Khaimah. Sharjah is the only emirate with borders on both the Persian Gulf and the Gulf of Oman. It is the third largest emirate with an area of 2,590 sq km (1,000 sq miles) and 30 km (17 miles) of coastline. The population of Sharjah is estimated at 435,000. Sharjah is known for its beautiful masterpieces of Arabic architecture, its *souks* and its fascinating mix of old and new. Sharjah has both oil and gas, allowing its people a high level of prosperity. Its capital city is located on the east coast and meets up with Dubai.

Umm Al-Qaiwain

Umm Al-Qaiwain (UAQ) has fewer than 80,000 residents and with less than 2 per cent of the total population it is the least populous of all the emirates. Its main industries are fishing and boat-building, with limited date production. Oil has not been found there. UAQ's attraction lies in its long clean beaches, an enclosed lagoon and public horse riding stables. This emirate has several housing developments planned over the next 15 years. Some of these developments are waterfront and will include mosques, schools, banks, shops, cafes, restaurants, marinas, horseback riding and cable cars.

BOUNDARY DISPUTES

Today, unclear boundaries exist with Oman and Saudi Arabia. Abu Dhabi and Saudi Arabia have a 1974 agreement settling their boundary dispute that has not been ratified by the UAE government and is not recognised by the Saudi Government. Oman and Abu Dhabi ratified an agreement in 2003 for their entire border, including the Musandam Peninsula and Al Madhad enclaves, but the agreement and maps have not been made public.

Of greater concern is the ongoing dispute with Iran over three islands in the Strait of Hormuz which it has shared with Sharjah since 1971. Iran has expanded its civilian and military presence on the disputed islands, prompting the UAE to press for sovereignty to the United Nations over the three islands.

CLIMATE

The climate of the UAE is uncomfortably hot and humid for about five months in the summer (mid-May to September). Temperatures are usually in the low 40s°C (from 104°F) but may sometimes reach higher than 50°C (122°F). Summer months are made even less pleasant by the coastal humidity which can reach 100 per cent. Before the development and the advent of air-conditioning, wind towers kept people cool. Many nationals have kept summer homes inland in Al-Ain or Liwa to escape the humidity. The mountains also afford some relief to people in the northern emirates, while air-conditioned houses, offices, shops and cars offer virtually non-stop respite from the heat to city residents. Ocean temperatures are high in summer at around 35°C (95°F), but they can go higher. When they do, the water is hotter than body temperature and a swim is no longer refreshing. Temperatures the rest of the year are quite pleasant. The days are clear and warm and the nights are cool. Inland temperatures can drop drastically at night to below 10°C (50°F) in winter.

The UAE is geologically stable and well-sheltered within the Persian Gulf. Thus, other than the relentless heat, it does not suffer major natural phenomena such as earthquakes, eruptions or typhoons. Occasionally the UAE does encounter very high winds. Newly-installed weather monitoring equipment at the airports confirms that the region experiences force one and two tornadoes.

Rainfall

The UAE averages less than 127 mm (5 inches) of rain a year. Rain usually falls during the winter months of October to March, with most rain falling in February. The rainfall can be dangerous when it is concentrated over a short space and time. The sand can absorb just enough to cement into a hard-packed floor. Water accumulates on the surface and as it increases it gains force until the earth cannot bear its weight and crumbles away. A canyon is then torn into the earth's surface. Water rushes down the new canyon, carrying with it anything in its path including people, animals, cars and houses. This type of canyon is called a *wadi*. Its newly-formed walls afford enough shade for vegetation to grow and it will often carry a permanent trickle of water in it. Very old, permanent *wadis* have settlements near them, and seeking newly-formed *wadis* is a source of entertainment now that four-wheel-drive cars make the trip across the desert fairly simple.

Heavy rainfall is dangerous in the cities because gutters and storm water drains have not been installed and standing water will quickly snarl traffic.

Although the average rainfall in the UAE is quite low, flooding can occur when sudden storms strike.

NATURE
Animals

Animals in the desert have adapted to survive in a harsh climate where food and water are scarce. The indigenous animals are domestic camels, cows, goats and donkeys and the wild animals are gazelles, oryx, foxes, wolves, hares and rodents. Most are light in colour to reflect the sun's rays and to blend in with their background. They rest in shade or burrow underground during the hot parts of the day, and hunt in the evening.

Birds migrate north in the summer and return in the winter. The most common reptiles to be found in the UAE are the spiney-tailed lizard, monitor lizard, sand viper, sand snake, and the Arabian rear-fanged snake, also called the False Cobra. These reptiles often match the colour of the sand to permit them to hide and hunt. Most of them prey small rodents and while their bite may sting, none of them are dangerously venomous. With the country's development, natural habitats are disappearing and the UAE government is establishing conservation areas to preserve unique species.

Plants

The region has a surprising number and variety of grass and plants which have adapted to growing in sand and on the hills. They do not grow tall, usually not more than half a metre, and many varieties are lower to the ground and are of a spreading variety. Trees grow between 3 m and 8 m high, the most common of these being the date palm. The stems of the date palm can be used for fuel, and leaves provide food for camels and sheep. The palm tree is known as the bride of the desert. It is one of the oldest trees and is certainly the most important. It provides shade, water, food, and material for housing, nets and boats.

Trees were numerous where water was stored underground, and as more trees grew around the area they formed an oasis. The Bedouin would settle around the oasis. They would install elaborate methods of irrigation based on astronomical calculations to regulate flow and these irrigation systems, called *falaj*, traced the underground water. Ground water was abundant in the Gulf region and Bedouin were renowned in their ability to detect it and drill accurate artesian wells. Many wells from long ago are still used today, particularly in the Hatta area. Desalination has surpassed the wells in producing sweet water by a factor of more than 12:1.

The occasional oasis belies the otherwise hostile environment of the desert.

ASTRONOMY

The Bedouin also used their knowledge of the stars in determining when to plant, where to go in the desert to find water, and to forecast the weather. The stars inspired folklore and poetry, and the navigation of ships depended on knowledge of the stars. 48 stars are today identified only by their Arabic names and these stars are critical to navigation. The moon is used in navigation and to determine the month's cycle as well as tidal movements. The sun tells the time of day and when to pray. Its position in the sky even helps determine when and how much water should be released from the *falaj* to cultivate the land.

The wind and the clouds guided sailing vessels and informed people of impending changes to the weather. The UAE is exposed to hot tropical winds and cold winds from the north. These winds continuously change direction, blowing from the north in winter but subject to change depending on time of day and atmospheric pressure. The morning can see a sea fog and spring and summer see sand storms. Knowledge of the winds is essential for fishing and sailing, and for citing which direction to pitch a tent, a house and even Dubai's Al Burj—a colossal skyscraper in progress.

THE EMIRATES THROUGH THE AGES
Archaeology

Archaeological findings reveal the presence of the first people to come to the UAE. The number of sites and their close proximity to one another show the significant volume in population on this peninsula. These findings date the sites, tell us of the level of advancement of the people, and also help Emiratis understand their past and how they have developed over time.

Umm Suqaim Mound is a historical site dating back to the first Bronze Age in 3000 BC. Here remnants of stone blocks, broken pottery, bronze and sea shells were found and they give evidence of the existence of a city whose people were likely involved in trade with ancient Indian and Iraqi civilisations.

The largest settlement on the Arabian Gulf coast was found 13 km northeast of Dubai. It is called Al Qusais Tombs, meaning Mound of Serpents. The find consists of 120 graves with skeletons, mosaic and stones decorated with serpents, and burial gifts. The place is thought to have been sacred, with serpents playing an important role in ceremonies. This civilisation dates between 2000 BC and 1000 BC.

Not far from this site, another one northwest of Dubai was discovered in 1968 and it dates to the first Islamic era between the 7th and 8th century. Evidence of a complete city was found, including a commercial *souk* and the Ruler's house, which had ten rooms on three sides all opened onto a large courtyard with the main entrance facing the sea.

Trade

Dubai has been the centre of trade for centuries. People came by sea and land to the open-air markets to buy fruit and vegetables, butter, charcoal and tobacco. Traditional boats called dhows brought supplies from other countries. Rice and spices came from India, dates and beans from Iran and cooking oil from East Africa. Shops carried canned goods, soap, pots and copper pans. Today the first, loudest and most sustained message that bombards visitors to Dubai is 'shop!'—a message based on a long and established tradition.

Early Contact

The UAE, conveniently located on a major trade route, has been inhabited since the third millennium BC. The first known group of people were the Umm An-Nar (Arabic for 'Mother of Fire') who settled on the island of Abu Dhabi and whose civilisation extended to the coast of Oman. They were probably fishermen, but little is actually known about them. They are thought to be unrelated to the famous Dilmun Empire, which was recently discovered to have been located nearby. Dilmun, developed during the Bronze Age from 3000 BC into one of the greatest trading groups in the ancient world. Their base is thought to have been Bahrain and they had a presence in the UAE. Also known as Telmun or Tylos, their location in Bahrain may have been the Garden of Eden.

After the Umm An-Nar civilisation came the Greeks who settled for a short time in the northern emirates for trade purposes. Trade continued in the area throughout the Bronze Age and into the Islamic era around AD 660, and then spread to all parts of the Arabian world, India and countries around the Mediterranean.

During the Middle Ages, the area formed part of the Kingdom of Hormuz. This group had control of the entrance to the Gulf and gave it the name Straits of Hormuz. The Portuguese followed and stayed from about AD 1500–1630. Because of its constant contact with other cultures through trade, influences are seen in many aspects of the Emirati culture, from everyday items to types of food and even genetic legacy. The Portuguese were driven out by forces both on land and at sea. The British and Dutch attacked with their fleets at sea while a tribe from Oman, called the Al-Busaid, came by land.

The Portuguese left their woodworking handicraft as a legacy. One may occasionally come across an old Portuguese chest in the market places of Oman or the UAE. These pieces can come with a very high price tag. Most likely though, the pieces are simply newly-constructed and made to look old.

Persia was also a contender for the land for a time in the mid-18th century. The region played a surprising role in the history of the US—Oman is reportedly the very first country to recognise the sovereignty of the US after it had won its independence from England.

British Presence

During the period from the 17th century into the 19th century, the British used their naval power to take a stronger hold of the area. While the British battled their way in by sea, two local tribes were gaining in size and power. One was the Qawasim tribe and the other the Bani Yas. Several of today's emirs (rulers) can trace their ancestors to these two tribes.

The Qawasim were seafarers who settled in what today is known as Ras al-Khaimah. They fought and pushed out the Persians, who were coming at them from Iran; and the Al-Busaids, the tribe invading from Oman. The Al-Busaids were fighting to keep the French out of Oman at the same time the Qawasims were pushing at their back door. The Al-Busaids enlisted the aid of the British to keep this new presence out. This move was perceived by the Qawasims as an alliance with the enemy, and they declared war on Britain, attacking British ships as they pleased. The British East India Company thought this was piracy and hence dubbed the area the Pirate Coast.

In the early 1800s, Britain retaliated with its own raids on the ships owned by the Qawasim but was unable to alter the situation. Then in 1820, the British came into the Gulf and destroyed or captured every Qawasim ship they could find and occupied Qawasim territory in Ras al-Khaimah and Persia (Iran). The British then imposed a peace treaty on the Arab tribes in the area. The treaty made it illegal for the Arabs to attack the British, but allowed the tribes to attack each other. The tribes did attack each other with a relish distasteful to the British, who repeatedly modified the treaty over the years in an effort to bring about a lasting peace. In 1853, the Treaty of Peace in Perpetuity was imposed, making the British arbitrators of disputes between the Sheikhs of warring tribes. The Pirate Coast became known

Feuds between warring tribes in the northern emirates continued as late as the mid-1980s. Some expatriates found themselves caught in gun battles of a 'Hatfield & McCoy' variety, and evidence for their tales could be found in bullet holes on their cars.

as the Trucial Coast after the ensuing truce interventions that followed.

The Oil Boom And Decolonisation

With the discovery of oil in the mid-20th century, Britain established an even stronger presence to protect this financial interest. Several British subjects were personally interested in the Arabs and their welfare. They lived with the Emiratis, wrote many books and generally educated much of the world about them. In 1968, in a political post-World War II climate favouring decolonisation, Britain pulled back and encouraged the Emiratis to form an independent country. The British withdrew politically and militarily, doing so with goodwill under a positive climate.

Britain's financial interests in the area remain strong and many of her subjects are gainfully employed in the UAE in the oil industry and other fields.

Negotiating A Way In

Another factor in Britain's withdrawal was the rise of Arab nationalism. The British had learned that military force was not effective with the Arabs and the way to guarantee British and other foreign enterprise in the Gulf was through negotiation and mutual respect of rights—not through military force. This applies too in daily life, as you will find that calmness and negotiation would serve you much better than losing your temper.

Modern History

In the 1940s the UAE signed two contracts with the British government, one to land planes and the other to search for oil. At the same time the Sheikhs encouraged development and kept taxes low. The first clinics and banks were established in this decade. However, the economy was negatively impacted by the introduction of cultured pearls by Japan into the world market, and also by the Second World War. Food supplies were difficult to come by.

During the 1950s governmental departments were forming. Police, courts, utilities, municipalities and airports were developed with proper governance. Attention was paid to town planning and establishing a road network, and trade in new industries such as gold added to the country's prosperity. Oil was first discovered in Abu Dhabi in 1958.

Political and economic growth was explosive in the 1960s. More and more oil was being discovered and the effort to put infrastructure in place paid off with the ability to move goods through airports, ports and across roads. Plans for the British to withdraw were underway, Dubai and Abu Dhabi united, and oil exports began.

In the 1970s the UAE came together as a federation. When the emirates formed their federation, the neighbouring countries of Bahrain and Qatar were invited to join, but both opted to remain independent. It was difficult to get all the emirates to agree on a constitution as well, so the Rulers of Abu Dhabi and Dubai formed a union between them and invited the other five emirates to join. Four of them did and the constitution was ratified on 2 December 1971 with the fifth emirate, Ras al-Khaimah, joining early in 1972. The country began using its wealth from oil to further build infrastructure, including ports, free zones, dry docks, concrete and aluminium plants, roads, tunnels, bridges and even water desalination plants.

In the 1980s and 1990s the country continued to develop and prosper. The population grew and with it service industries blossomed. Thousands and thousands of housing projects were completed, airports were expanded and recreational and sporting facilities were added with an eye looking toward international tourism.

LEADERSHIP
The First Ruler Of The New Country
The late HH President Sheikh Zayed bin Sultan Al Nahyan, Ruler of Abu Dhabi, came to power in Abu Dhabi in 1966 and was the country's founding President in 1971 until his death in November 2004. He had succeeded his older brother, Sheikh Shakhbut ibn Sultan Al Nahyan who ruled Abu Dhabi until 1966. Sheikh Shakhbut was a micromanager who hoarded his money and distrusted banks. In August

1966, a council of the ruling family held a bloodless coup and replaced Shakhbut with the more progressive Sheikh Zayed, whom they thought would be more capable in dealing with the rapid changes occurring due to the export of oil.

Sheikh Zayed established a government structure and initiated large development projects. As Britain ended its protectorate over the Trucial States, Sheikh Zayed led the formation of the federation whose rulers elected him to five-year terms as President of the UAE in 1971, 1976, 1981, 1986, 1991, 1996, and 2001.

One of the means to a stable economy is a stable political system. Having the same ruler since inception, and later on a smooth transition to Sheikh Zayed's son Sheikh Khalifa has helped. There was international speculation upon Sheikh Zayed's death in 2004 that the rulers of the other emirates might vie for power but this did not happen. The Emiratis have a deep respect for the past and history, and recognise that their strength and prosperity have come from being united and that they continue to benefit from presenting a united front.

The late UAE President, Sheikh Zayed bin Sultan Al Nahyan.

Foresight In Education

Sheikh Zayed began a campaign to educate his people before the emirates even formed to become a country. Upon request, Kuwait, Egypt and Qatar sent the Emirati Sheikhs money and teachers to establish their first schools in the 1950s. In the 1960s, as students began to graduate from these schools, they were sent abroad for university education. These students were all male. When they returned, they headed the country's new police force, municipality, department of education and such. Other countries continued to send more teachers to the area and the Emiratis were able to further develop their educational system.

Since the population of Emiratis is so small and their rate of development so great, women are needed to help run the country. In this, Sheikh Zayed firmly believed in educating the Emirati women. The Emirates' first university opened in 1972, consisting of a separate women's campus. The quality of education at the university is improving every year and has quite a good reputation. Muslim parents from all over the Middle East send their daughters to schools in the UAE, where they have the option of cloistering the girls behind walls without access to members of the opposite sex, drugs or anything else that might affect their reputation. Emirati women are welcome in the workforce and may be placed in high management positions where they are less likely to come into contact with men or be caught in situations that might compromise their reputation.

The literacy rate among UAE women was just over 22 per cent in 1980 and has risen to almost 90 per cent today, in line with the rate of literacy of the entire population. Higher literacy rates and education among women equate to more women in the workforce. This development has been driven by strong incentives from the government for women to pursue their education and by innovative new policies to enhance women's role in public life. Adult literacy classes are available for the Emiratis. Of adults taking literacy courses,

Elderly citizens of the UAE are the most likely to be illiterate because schooling and literacy programs were not widely available during their youth. Older adults who are not literate are eligible for free education classes.

women outnumber men. The UAE leads all other Arab countries in education, and is expected to reach 100 per cent literacy within the next five years.

Education has continued to be a primary development goal. It is an important force in accelerating cultural and political change. This has been proven true for many countries and is doing so in the UAE. In the past, the teacher was the main element in maintaining traditions. Now, the teacher, who often comes from abroad, is the agent of change.

Standard Of Living

Sheikh Zayed won his people's loyalty by using oil revenues to raise living standards and by providing UAE citizens with free education, medical care, housing and infrastructure; and by sharing responsibilities of his new government with his family members and the youth of the country. His popularity permeated every aspect of life. Businesses large and small, government or private, continue to post his picture in the front office, and nationals and non-nationals alike speak respectfully and lovingly of him.

The BCCI Affair

One blot on Sheikh Zayed's record was the controversy surrounding the Bank of Credit and Commerce International (BCCI), an institution Sheikh Zayed helped found in 1972 with Aghan Hasan Abadi, a Pakistani banker. This bank was engaged in what is known as a 'Ponzi scheme' where abnormally high returns are paid to investors out of money paid in by subsequent investors rather than from net revenues generated by any real business. BCCI was found to be an organised crime syndicate guilty of bribery, money laundering, arms trafficking, prostitution and supporting terrorism. In 1990 a Price Waterhouse audit of BCCI showed a loss of hundreds of millions of dollars at which point Sheikh Zayed paid the loss in exchange for increasing Abu Dhabi's shareholding to 78 per cent. The bank subsequently failed in 1991 as layers of deception came to light. Sheikh Zayed's name though was never directly linked to the crime and schemes.

Sheikh Zayed's legacy of religious tolerance, use of diplomacy and dialogue to settle disputes, turning the desert into green, advocating for women's rights, giving to poorer nations and improving the living conditions of the country's residents continues today with his successors. Sheikh Zayed was admired not only at home, but by the rest of the world as a moderate and gentle ruler. The world has lost a truly great man.

The Federal Government

The UAE is a federation of seven independent emirates, each with its own ruler. 'Emir' or 'Sheikh' are words meaning prince. They are used to refer to the rulers, and the honorific 'Sheikh' is preferred in the UAE ('Sheikha' for the wives of the rulers). Of late, HH for His Highness is frequently used as part of the title.

Present Rulers

The current rulers of the emirates are:

- HH President Sheikh Khalifa bin Zayed Al Nahyan, Ruler of Abu Dhabi
- HH Vice-President, Prime Minister Sheikh Mohammed bin Rashid Al Maktoum, Ruler of Dubai
- HH Dr. Sheikh Sultan bin Mohammed Al Qasimi, Ruler of Sharjah
- HH Sheikh Saqr bin Mohammed Al Qasimi, Ruler of Ras al-Khaimah
- HH Sheikh Hamad bin Mohammed Al Sharqi, Ruler of Fujairah
- HH Shiekh Rashid bin Ahmad Al Mu'alla, Ruler of Umm al-Quiwain
- HH Sheikh Humaid bin Rashid Al Nuaimi, Ruler of Ajman

The federal government (called the Supreme Council), led by HH President Sheikh Khalifa bin Zayed Al Nahyan, Ruler of Abu Dhabi and oldest son of the late Sheikh Zayed bin Sultan al Nahyan, controls the country's foreign affairs, defence and the federation's economic and social development. The Supreme Council is a constitutional republic headed by a president and council of ministers with Islamic ideals and beliefs providing customs, laws and practices. Critical to the designation of a constitutional republic is the election of officials; the separation of executive, legislative and judicial powers into distinct branches so that no individual or group has absolute power; and a constitution existing that limits the government's power and which is subject to judicial review. This is certainly the direction in which the UAE is moving but some of the emirates still have elections where the vote is cast by the ones who have been appointed by those in power rather than by the people.

Below the Supreme Council is the Cabinet. Most of the Cabinet posts are held by Abu Dhabi and Dubai, in consideration of having contributed the most money to the federal government. In addition to the Supreme Council and the Cabinet there is a National Council made up of 40 members. Some emirates vote their members in and some have members who are appointed by the Sheikhs, and appointments tend to go to family members based on relationships and favours. The National Council advises the other two political entities but cannot overrule them.Abu Dhabi has hired external political consultants to further improve their governance and progress towards a free and open society.

PROBLEMS OF MODERNISATION

Money has made life easy for the Emiratis in some respects, but this has brought with it incumbent problems. Money from oil has provided the Emiratis with comfortable, air-conditioned housing, cars and office jobs. The Emiratis are now growing up without learning to endure desert conditions. When the oil runs out (oil reserves are expected to last about 90 more years), the money will run out as well. Emiratis will not be able to readjust to traditional life in the desert.

The government has embarked upon a massive effort to educate its people and promote tourism to prevent this eventuality. The Emiratis have financially diversified, such that their investments around the world will support them. The government is also working very hard to convert the desert back into cultivatable land.

A further complication is a fast approaching end to fresh water supply. Even if the Emiratis wished to return to a traditional lifestyle, they would not be able to because of the shortage of fresh water. Demand for water is and has been growing by 10 per cent a year. The UAE produces 12.5 per cent of the world's total desalinated water and this production accounts for 70 per cent of the country's sweet water use. This water is subsidised by the government and in return, the government asks of the people to conserve water.

Westerners have brought in their expertise and their non-Muslim values. Since the Emiratis still need the foreigners' expertise and want their tourism dollars, they are tolerant and accommodating of foreign behaviours and values. The five-star hotels are the expatriates' playgrounds. Muslim Arabs are not allowed in parts of these hotels such as the bars, but some nationals do end up frequenting them.

As one solution to curb the proliferation of non-Muslim values on the locals, the Emiratis are trying to change the make-up of the population by attempting to hire more Muslim Arabs (Lebanese, Egyptians, and Palestinians) whose values are more aligned to theirs.

In the past, families were always together in the desert. They often had little to do, and hence much time was spent enjoying each other's company. Now fathers are often away on business and servants do any work that needs to be done at home. The women thus shop a lot or watch television, although this has also been a benefit in that it has contributed to women's pursuit of higher education.

Many men, having little responsibility and plenty of money, drive brand new SUVs around the desert or sit and talk in a shady area. The lack of responsibility or need to be productive can result in low self-esteem and indulgence in vices. To combat this problem, the government has an ongoing campaign of marketing pride for traditional values, and pushing its citizens to be more actively involved in governing the country.

The government has also sought the very best organisations in the world to enhance health, education and cultural resources so that its citizens may have access to the best education and be prepared for jobs in all sectors. The government then pays them extraordinarily well as they enter the workforce. At the same time, it increasingly holds the nationals accountable for doing their very best in their jobs.

Corruption

Corruption, financial mismanagement and lack of transparency constitute a very important challenge for development in the UAE. Instances of those in government positions such as construction inspectors asking for favours in return for approval are not uncommon. These result in delays or contracts going only to those who are willing to bribe.

The construction sector is the segment of society most likely to uncover corruption because it is so noticeable when a crane topples or a bridge collapses. To its credit, the UAE has one of the lowest corruption levels among all Arab countries and further progress is being pursued through federal legislation, political reforms, maintaining democracy and improved administrative performance with enforced accountability and punishment.

Construction Quality

Most of the country's hard labour is carried out by Pakistanis, Afghanis, Indians and Baluchistanis. What this results in is men doing work for which they may not have much understanding. For example, the man doing the electrical wiring for a newly-constructed building is likely to have lived much of his life without electricity and the man driving a taxi may have never even been a passenger in a car until he came to this country. Brand new buildings may have satellite reception while cable for telephones might be forgotten. The work must then be redone. While the world is amazed at the marvel of the fast pace of development in the UAE, those within the UAE tend to be astonished instead by the questionable workmanship, oversight and codes.

Crime

'It is proper that a private harm
be borne to avert a public harm.'
—UAE law, Article 105

The UAE is thought to have one of the lowest crime rates in the world. About 1.5 per cent of the UAE's population is impacted by crime each year., but since the government does not release crime statistics, this is difficult to confirm. One thing is certain—mundane and petty crime is on the rise, judging by accounts in the newspapers and tales told by the general public.

The UAE judicial system acts severely against criminals. An expatriate, once convicted of a crime, receives a harsh sentence and once this is served, is deported, thereby eliminating the incidence of recidivism.

Violent crime is still rare. There has been a steady increase in reported drug smuggling, dealing and usage, with the government stepping up security at ports of entry. Penalties for drug crimes are harsh and strictly enforced, and a barrier at the Omani border has been constructed to stem the flow of illicit drugs there.

Crime tends to take place among the large expatriate labour workforce, leaving Western expatriates and UAE nationals unharmed. Westerners however are lulled into a false sense of security and may not take general precautions, leaving them vulnerable to theft, and the women vulnerable to sexual assault.

Drug Trafficking

An estimated 15 to 20 per cent of the opium produced in Afghanistan flows through Iran into the Gulf. The UAE is vulnerable to drug trafficking of all kinds as it is close to drug-producing countries, has large foreign communities and a 500 km (311 mile) coastline. While the UAE is able to prevent drugs from entering the country at airports, having similar strict checks for land and sea entry is much harder to achieve. When authorities crack down on trafficking in nearby countries, smugglers are forced to find new routes to Europe and North America, and the UAE serves them well. Dubai is strategically located and with its booming economy and high individual income, it is a potential market for a highly organised drug network. The UAE is very serious about drug crimes and advocates severe punishment, introducing the death penalty for trafficking in 1995, which is enforced strictly. Dubai authorities are gaining considerable skill in combating traffickers but the Arab world has a long way to go towards sharing information about drug cartels so they can destroy their networks before they get established.

THE EMIRATIS

CHAPTER 3

'You need a brother, without one you're like
a person rushing to battle without a weapon.'
—Arabic proverb

POPULATION

One of the most unique aspects of the UAE's population is its rapid increase. Prior to 1960, the population ranged between 80,000 and 95,000. Sources internal to the UAE estimate the total population in 2006 to be 4.9 million, while external sources give an estimate of 4.6 million. This figure is 50 to 60 times larger than that of half a century ago, due mainly to the immigration of foreign workers.

The UAE has one of the highest living standards in the world and its economic opportunities attract Indians, Pakistanis, Bangladeshis, Nepalese and Sri Lankans. Population of hte countries in the region, including the UAE, is expected to double by 2050, based on current estimates.

UAE's Population Distribution

The population is distributed among the emirates as follows: 38.8 per cent Abu Dhabi; 31 per cent Dubai; 15.3 per cent Sharjah; 6 per cent Ajman; 4.5 per cent Ras Al-Khaimah; 2.8 per cent Al-Fujairah; and 1.6 per cent Umm Al-Quwain. The bulk of the population live in cities. with only 12 per cent living in towns or oilfield camps scattered throughout the country.

The population of the UAE is one of the most diverse in the Middle East. UAE government estimates put the national population at nearly 22 per cent, but non-UAE sources estimate this to be more modest at 15 per cent. Arabs from other nations comprise 20 per cent. These Arab nationals come from 20 nations including Palestine, many who have come as political refugees or migrant workers. Indian, Bangladeshi and Pakistani nationals are the largest expatriate community at nearly 55 per cent, while the Westerners and East Asians make up the remaining 10 per cent of the population.

Gender

Another unique aspect of the UAE's population is its unnatural gender distribution, with more than twice the number of men than women, particularly among the working aged population of 15–65 where 70 per cent of the population fall. The UAE nationals have the most even gender balance with males representing 50.7 per cent of the group and females constituting 49.3 per cent. The gender distribution among non-UAE residents is 72 per cent male and 28 per cent female.

The UAE's gender imbalance is the greatest among any nation in the world including any of the Gulf Cooperation Council (GCC) nations of Qatar, Kuwait, Bahrain, Oman, and Saudi Arabia.

THE WORKING POPULATION

Not all people are equal. Status is awarded according to nationality and is portrayed most obviously in work opportunities. Low-status jobs involve manual labour. White-collar work is awarded higher status because of the desire not to have 'clean hands' blackened by work. The subtle preference for light skin in so many parts of the world holds true too in the UAE. While the persistence of racism anywhere is strange, it is even more bizarre in the UAE where this is juxtaposed against so many unexpected levels of tolerance where skin colour or nationality are not factors.

Work is largely carried out by the middle class. The government has initiatives to nationalise the workforce, with strides being made in some sectors, primarily governmental. Government jobs are well-paid and almost exclusive to Emiratis. In late 2007, all government employees received a 70 per cent salary increase.

Do Your Job!

HH Sheikh Mohammed bin Rashid Al Maktoum, Vice President and Prime Minister of the UAE, and Ruler of Dubai, is a man who strives for excellence. He was rumoured to have fired two government employees who were not at their job when they should have been. This unprecedented move is a message to UAE citizens they are expected to participate in the building of their great nation and they will be handsomely rewarded for doing so to the best of their abilities. Sheikh Mohammed is sending this message on every front, and it is appreciated by nationals and non-nationals alike.

The Bedouin

The Emiratis were (and a few still are) a nomadic group of people called Bedouin. They travelled in family groups, tending their herds of sheep, goats and camels, raiding other tribes and seeking sources of fresh water. These tribes ranged in size from a few to thousands. They grouped together for protection from other warring tribes. Contact with another Bedouin tribe could be cause for celebration or dispute over territorial boundaries.

The Bedouin's easily-constructed houses were made

The Emiratis are very proud of their Bedouin heritage, from their customs to their strength of character and their renowned hospitality. They are very sociable, generous and patient—values that have arisen out of their very harsh existence.

from palm fronds or blankets forming a tent with an open side, and their possessions were few and light to enable them to travel quickly. Carpets were laid on the sand to serve as the floor. Camels and goats from their herds provided milk, meat and wool for shelter and clothing. Meat came also from gazelles the men hunted or from the bustard, an indigenous bird the men caught with the aid of their falcons. Dates were taken from date palms growing in *wadis*.

Some Bedouin tribes settled in oases, near water where they could grow their food and raise their flocks. Their homes were more permanently made with date palm trunks, fronds and mud. Houses were small and rectangular with a short, narrow wooden door for an entry way. These narrow doors made it difficult for an unwanted intruder to force his entry. Food was still provided by the Bedouin's herds and by hunting, but an irrigation system called a *falaj* was also developed and these more permanent settlers began growing some crops.

Women were respected and had their own special rights. They worked beside their husbands and were free to manage their own affairs. The tribes were divided into branches, sub-branches and families with relatives living together—a community bonded by blood ties and marriage that enabled them to defend themselves, survive and preserve their social customs.

Royal Families And Upper Class

Out of these Bedouin tribes have come today's royalty. Royal families in each emirate are quite large and of high profile in the news. Their wealth is practically obscene and seemingly capable of moving the earth. Today, most of the UAE nationals are considered upper class, a small percentage is poor and very few are members of the middle class.

There are still Bedouin in the UAE today. They sometimes roam the desert on the backs of their camels but may also tend their herds in a Toyota Land Cruiser. Most likely though, they have hired subcontinent labourers to tend the herds.

Camel racing is popular amongst the Emiratis and the trade in racing camels is a source of income for those who maintain a Bedouin lifestyle.

They earn a healthy living by raising camels for racing. The government often fronts the cash prizes at these races.

Bedouin have not entirely given up raiding—they breed their camels with herds they come across in the desert. This is considered raiding as camels are very difficult to breed for two reasons: the male camel is highly selective, and the female has a long gestation of 12–14 months bringing just one camel to birth each time. Wild camels do not exist in the UAE; all are owned. However, they are allowed to freely graze anywhere. You will encounter them on forays away from the cities. They are fairly docile animals and very well-protected by law. In fact, if you hit one while out driving in the desert, you will meet the Bedouin owner in court.

Non-Gulf Arabs: Seven Trades But No Luck

The non-Gulf Arabs, who come from Egypt, Syria, Palestine, Lebanon, Jordan and Algeria, to name a few, tend to be well-educated. They are often fluent in English, French as well as Arabic, as these languages are widely spoken in their home countries. They are also a highly-skilled group. Many of them have their own businesses in the UAE which they may own outright if they began those businesses a long time back. Nowadays it is a requirement for an Emirati to own at least 51 per cent of a business, unless the business is located in a free zone, in which case 100 per cent foreign ownership is allowed. Still other members of this group are professors at the university, doctors or some other type of professional.

Non-Gulf Arabs are as family-oriented as the Emiratis are. Friends and spouses are usually met or made through family connections and socialising tends to be in the home at large family gatherings. However, this is not possible for them in the UAE where only their nuclear family is present. As a result, this group may feel quite isolated. Some of these Arabs are Muslim and some are Christian. The men often choose to wear Western dress. The women may also wear Western dress, though it is very conservative—long skirts, high necklines and full length sleeves.

> Non-Gulf Arab women cover their heads if they are Muslim. Their head scarves are different from the Emiratis' in that they are white or multi-coloured and multi-patterned instead of black. If you pay close attention, you can even notice differences in the way the head scarf is worn.

Members of this group have no rights to citizenship in the UAE and many have children who are entering adulthood and have known no other home. These children are usually welcome in their parents' home country where they have citizenship but no affinity. They speak Arabic as a first language and are often fluent in English. They attend school with Emirati children but while the UAE government pays for the education of the Emirati children, the non-gulf Arab families pay out of pockets for their children's education. An entire generation of children is now entering young adulthood and the complexity of their situation is a burgeoning social issue. The UAE government is carefully considering extending citizenship for those born and raised in the UAE, and does provide educational scholarships to local universities for many of them

Westerners

Many Western expatriates belong to the middle class due to their professional knowledge, experience, expertise, education and income. This middle class membership is financial for the expatriates and has no relation to Emirati society. Workers in this class are generally provided housing, an annual repatriation ticket and other benefits. If retirement benefits are not available, an employer may provide one month's pay for every year of service. This pay will come in one lump sum when service is terminated.

Housing can be ridiculously large for single Westerners or even for families as Westerners tend to have fewer children than Emirati families do, and housing is built to the Emirati cultural reality. A forgivable loan for furnishing a home and an interest-free loan to purchase a car might also be part of the package. A minimum salary must be earned in order for an employee to sponsor a spouse and children to live in the UAE. Westerners generally earn enough to qualify. Social life is multicultural and includes a variety of sports, parties and events.

The majority of Westerners in the UAE come from England. Others come from the US, Australia, Ireland, New Zealand, Scotland, Canada and Africa. A few come from non English-speaking countries in Europe. Some enjoy the lifestyle, the weather and the generous salaries so much, they make the UAE their new home, though citizenship is never extended because it is only available to Emiratis and their children. They become diplomats, teach English, staff hospitals, run and maintain oil rigs, manage businesses, work in the import-export field, provide a range of professional services from counselling to massage, and give training of all kinds. Generally their occupations require special skill, training or education and a fluent, native-like command of English.

They tend to be well-salaried, with housing and expenses paid for by their companies. They work reasonable hours and have at least a month of vacation time each year, often more. They have an abundance of leisure time and with the expansion of the tourism industry, there are endless opportunities to recreate.

Labourers

Labourers form the largest group of people in the UAE. They come from Pakistan, Afghanistan, India and other South Asia countries. Almost all the labourers are men and this accounts for the great gender imbalance found in the UAE.

The labourers earn well by the standards of their home countries, but are poor in the UAE. They clean the streets, construct the buildings, water the fields, tend the animals and hire themselves out. They do not earn enough money to support their families in the UAE. However, they do make three or four times as much in the UAE as they could in their home countries. Several men share accommodation, or even live under the bridges they are building. They pool resources to make their meals and ride bikes, walk and take buses to save as much as possible. Safety concerns are also high for this population and it is far too common to read about things such as bridges collapsing and killing workers.

It is common for men in the better paid service jobs to return home for a month-long visit once every two years. Taxi drivers send their salary home and live only on their tips. They live like this for years, often until they are old men.

Foreign labourers live in makeshift accomodation, but make more money than they could earn in their own countries.

They can then go home and enjoy the fruits of their labour among the children and grandchildren they have sired on their few vacations home. It is the practice in some cultures for a brother to sire the children in their absence.

The Ministry of Labour sets a minimum one-year term of employment before an employee may transfer to another employer so that the company may recoup its investment in the employee. If an employee is in a bad situation, they are stuck that first year or they will be banned permanently from working in the UAE. In fact, they must have a 'no-objection certificate' (NoC) to transfer to another employer. Some employers, even entire industries, will never provide NoCs as a collective agreement so as to discourage competition.

Seeking Employment In The UAE

There are many questionable employers and employment practices when working overseas. If considering employment abroad, search the Internet for blogs on a prospective employer, ask the employer for contacts of current employees and permission to talk to them, and never pay visa charges or other expenses incurred by the company to employ you as this is against the UAE labour law.

It is also against the law for the employer to keep an employee against his or her will, though this happens frequently. A labour complaint can be filed but when the complaint is against an Emirati, the situation is complicated not by the law, which is clear, but by the reality which has an awful lot to do with the Emirati's position and power or kickbacks they are receiving. Those with little education are least able to advocate for themselves and suffer the greatest abuses.

Working conditions are particularly hard on those who work in the construction industry. Their hours are long, they are often made to work in the heat of the day, and pay can be sporadic, making them little more than indentured servants forced to live in substandard conditions.

Conditions have become so bad that this group does strike and the UAE government committed itself to 'study the situation', resulting in some positive changes. The government now requires employers to deposit their workers' pay directly into the bank. In this way, the government can monitor whether any deductions have been taken by the employer, an illegal but common practice.

Providing workers health insurance became mandatory as of 2008, and a minimum wage is under consideration. The government has built some new modern dormitories and provides a court where workers can voice their grievances. As of this writing the government has yet to crack down on companies violating labour laws. The desire for cheap labour works to the Emiratis' advantage in the development of their country, but this has damaged its image, and experts who analyse political and economic stability downgrade the UAE because the underlying anger of a significant portion of its population makes it an easy target for terrorists to exploit.

Work opportunities in India are changing dramatically due to the boom in construction there. If workers can earn as much in India where the cost of living is lower and they can be with their families, the urge to migrate to the Gulf for better opportunities will diminish. As the number of job seekers goes down, competition and the work situation for them in the UAE should improve.

Highly-educated subcontinent citizens have jobs requiring skill and education. Their earnings may be high enough for them to bring their families along with them. They may even have established several generations of family in the UAE. They command respect, mix well with Westerners and retain many of their values. These include the continued tradition of arranged marriages (much in keeping with the host culture) and to educate children according to the standards of the home country, even if it means sending them abroad to study.

Illegal Immigrants

Many of the labourers, approximately 335,000 in 2006, are illegal immigrants and must take whatever work they can get. Illegal aliens have been tolerated for periods of time in the past, but the UAE has cracked down on them significantly, offering a period of amnesty for the illegals to get their passports and leave the country or transfer to a new employer. Illegal immigrants are not wanted as they endanger national security, threaten the stability of the economy and labour market, and cause harm to the nation's reputation with the international community.

The government has enacted laws to safeguard security and privacy. Every country is moving at some rate towards such modern technologies with privacy and security of the systems being of concern to most people. Privacy is not a guarantee in the UAE. In the early 1990s phone conversations were occasionally monitored and access to the Internet was controlled. As satellite systems came available and people were able to circumvent internal government systems and access information from all over the world, the government progressed with the times.Instead of policing everyone all the time, illegal activity is sought, monitored, and handled efficiently and unequivocally.

The Emirates Identity Authority (EIA) is charged with developing and implementing an identity management system for citizens and residents of the UAE. An individual's photograph, fingerprint and e-signature are logged and the person is issued a smart card which serves as a driver's license, the right to work and to obtain health services. The card may also be able to handle money much like a credit card. Not only are these cards intended to police and prevent illegal immigration, they will serve as the data collection portal for a database to measure economic, demographic and social characteristics of the country with accuracy and speed to guide the government in providing more efficient services.

Amnesty International

The Amnesty International annual report on human rights progress in the UAE has been improving slightly and the Emiratis do pay attention to it. For example, there is now a federal law against human trafficking, with penalties ranging from one year to life imprisonment. How widely it is enforced is another matter. The report typically downgrades the UAE for the imposition of the death penalty and cruel punishments without charges or proper judicial procedures, forced returns to home countries and persecution of human rights activists. Such incidences are few and when Amnesty International brings public pressure to bear on an incident, the Emiratis tend to respond humanely.

SOCIAL WELFARE

Social security benefits are available to the nationals who are unable to benefit from the UAE's prosperity. These include widowed and divorced national women who were previously married to foreigners, expatriate husbands who are married to UAE women, those who are disabled or handicapped, seniors, orphans, single women, married students, estranged wives, those who are bankrupt or insolvent and relatives of those who are jailed. The number of people dependent on the system has declined, but the cost to administer the system has risen dramatically as the cost of living increases. The government gives generously to recipients who are Emirati.

Disabled And Handicapped

The disabled and handicapped have traditionally been hidden from the public as something shameful because this is a culturally held belief. Progress in incorporating them into society has been slow, with change taking place most quickly in the big cities. Airports are equipped for the disabled. At the airport a specifically-modified taxi can be requested from the Transport Authority. The Dubai Department of Tourism and Commerce Marketing Group (DTCM) formed the Special Needs People Tourism Working Committee to improve and plan greater handicap accessibility around the city of Dubai.

Improvements have been made to the accessibility to heritage sites, schools, shopping centres and cinemas. Most five-star hotels and restaurants are wheelchair-accessible.

The UAE government has established care centres for those with special needs, expanded and enhanced vocational training programmes for the handicapped, and set a job quota for them. These are primarily for the estimated 5,500 disabled UAE nationals, but dependents of some residents are also able to use the services.

RELIGION

Over 75 per cent of the population of the UAE is Muslim. Muslims follow the religion of Islam, an Arabic root word meaning 'peace' and 'submission'. Islam teaches that one can only find peace in one's life by submitting to Almighty God (Allah) in heart, soul and deed. The same Arabic root word is in the universal Muslim greeting, '*salaam alaykum*', meaning 'peace be upon you'. It is estimated that one in five people in the world are Muslim and that fewer than 15 per cent of Muslims are Arab. The UAE's constitution declares that Islam is the official religion of all seven of the constituent emirates of the federal union. Muslims are expressly prohibited from converting to other religions, but conversion by non-Muslims to Islam is viewed favourably.

Sunni vs Shia

The Emiratis are predominantly of the Sunni sect, as are 85 per cent of all Muslims. Sunni and Shia Muslims share the most fundamental Islamic beliefs and articles of faith. Their differences stem from politics dating back to the death of the Prophet Muhammad, and the question of who was to take over the leadership of the Muslim nation. These political differences have spawned a number of varying practices and positions which now carry spiritual significance.

Sunni Muslims agree with the position taken by many of the Prophet's companions that the new leader should be elected from among those capable of the job. This is what was done, and the Prophet Muhammad's close friend and advisor, Abu Bakr, became the first Caliph of the Islamic nation. The word 'Sunni' in Arabic comes from a word meaning 'one who follows the traditions of the Prophet'.

The Shia Muslims believe leadership should have stayed within the Prophet's family and following the Prophet Muhammad's death, leadership should have passed directly to his cousin and son-in-law, Ali. The Shia Muslims follow a line of imams whom they believe have been appointed by the Prophet Muhammad or God himself. 'Shia' is shortened from 'Shia-t-Ali' or 'the Party of Ali', and in Arabic means 'supportive party'.

The question of political leadership impacted some aspects of spiritual life and brought about different practices over time. Shia Muslims believe that the imam is sinless by nature, and that his authority is infallible as it comes directly from God. Sunni Muslims do not venerate imams. Nor do they believe in a hereditary privileged class. Shia Muslims felt animosity towards some of Prophet Muhammad's companions because of their positions and actions over the question of leadership following the Prophet's death. Many of these companions narrated traditions about the Prophet's life and spiritual practice which Shia Muslims rejected. This gave rise to the differences in religious practice including prayer, fasting, and pilgrimage to list a few. Any practices described in this book pertain to Sunni Muslims.

Mosques

Mosques are the centre of religious and cultural life in the UAE. In the past they also served as schools where children learned to recite the Qur'an from memory. Now Islamic studies are mandatory for citizen children attending public schools and for Muslim children attending private schools. Religious instruction in non-Muslim religions is not permitted in public schools. Non-Muslims are not permitted to enter mosques in the UAE except during special times when tours are organised. A central federal regulatory authority distributes weekly guidance to imams regarding the content of religious sermons.

There is supposed to be a mosque within five minutes' walking distance of every male Muslim. There are an amazing number of mosques in the UAE and it is likely this goal has been achieved. The King Faisal Mosque in Sharjah is the largest mosque in the UAE and can hold up to 3,000 worshippers. Al Bidyah Mosque in Fujairah, built of mud and bricks is thought to be the oldest mosque in the UAE, built in AD 1446.

Bounties Are From God

Religion and daily life are practically synonymous in the UAE. Religion informs behaviour and is interspersed in the language through frequent expressions making reference to God. Religious practices may feel invasive the way they are widely and publicly practised. For example, prayer call will wake you every morning between 4:30 am and 5:00 am,

King Faisal Mosque. The large number of mosques in the UAE makes it possible for every male Muslim to attend prayer calls and services.

government workers will disappear in the middle of a transaction to pray, and the attempt to get a commitment to a future obligation will be placed in God's hands. The more you understand the Emiratis' religion, the more tolerant you will be and you will be less likely to cause offence yourself.

Islam guides every aspect of the Emiratis' lives. Care must be taken to avoid causing offence by saying or acting in ways that go against Islam. This becomes easier in a very short time once you become accustomed to societal norms. Emiratis are amazingly tolerant of other religions (with the exception of Judaism, as discussed later in this chapter). They respect the beliefs others hold and are impressed by religious devotion. They do not, however, comprehend a lack of religious faith. So while Emiratis may curiously interrogate you about your beliefs, keep it to yourself if you are atheist or agnostic. They don't understand and may express shock at such a declaration.

Expressing an interest in Islam is always appreciated. Emiratis know quite a bit about Christianity and are amazed at how little Christians know about Islam. They are happy to educate the uninformed and an information exchange

Conversion Attempts

For the Emiratis, the more they like you, the more they may try to convert you because they are deeply concerned about your prospects for meeting God in the end. It is well-meant.

may turn into an attempted conversion. The Emiratis love their religion and God. Their enthusiasm and religious fervour is overflowing. Still, they are concerned about not offending you and may feel bad if their enthusiasm causes you discomfort. Their tolerance of you and desire to make you comfortable inform their face-to-face interactions with you.

Muslims view their religion as a continuation of Christianity, but see Islam as the one true faith. The reason Islam is viewed as a continuation of Christianity is due to the significant similarities between the two religions. They share the concept of a Heaven and a Hell with a Satan figure presiding over Hell, and God (Allah) in Heaven. Muslims and Christians believe that on the final day when God judges mankind, each person will receive their just reward or punishment as they deserve, based on the way they lived their life. Followers of both religions recognise many prophets in common in the histories of their religions, many of whom are the same for both religions. These prophets had to repeatedly teach the people through the centuries because the people continually strayed from their teachings.

People of each faith, Christian and Muslim, believe only the doctrines of their faith are true and valid. They believe that there is little hope for those who have heard the doctrine and do not believe. Muslims believe as Christians do that Jesus was born of the Virgin Mary (Miriam in Arabic) and that he performed miracles. They believe as Christians do that he raised the dead, fed the poor and cured the sick. Where they differ in their belief, and this is pivotal, is that they see Jesus as a prophet and not as the Son of God. Muslims do not believe Jesus was crucified but that it was someone else who died on the cross. Christians believe in a Holy Trinity of God, His Son Jesus, and the Holy Spirit. Muslims believe there is only God. Thus, while Christians can pray to Jesus to intercede with God on their behalf, Muslims pray directly to God only. Emiratis are particularly curious about this point and if you

are interested in taking on the argument, you will need to be well-read and knowledgeable or else risk losing face. If you would prefer not to be engaged in a religious debate, state that you do not care to discuss your religious beliefs.

In the West, Church and State have pretty well been separated. This is not the case in the UAE where religion is the source of law and not long ago was even the sole resource for educators. Muslims do not wish for any reduction of the role of religion in their lives.

Paradise

Muslims are very focused on the afterlife. They believe they will go to a paradise with lush gardens, tall green trees and flowing waters. In many ways they try to create that paradise here on earth. Al-Ain, the garden city of the UAE, is heavily watered to ensure palm trees grow throughout the city. The trees do indeed grow, serving the purpose of providing shade and keeping the sand out of the city. It may be hard to comprehend how a country fast running out of fresh water and depleting its water table daily could continue to water this vision of paradise, but this is why.

The Five Pillars Of Islam

The five pillars of Islam are the main rules Muslims follow in their lifetimes. These pillars are the profession of faith (*iman*), prayer (*saleh*), fasting (*sawm*), alms-giving (*zakah*) and a pilgrimage to Mecca (*Hajj*). The first pillar, the Declaration of Faith, states, 'There is no God but Allah and Muhammad is the messenger of God.' This declaration is made when professing faith or converting to Islam. When converting, the declaration must be made in front of two male Muslims.

Salah is the name for the obligatory prayers that are performed five times a day, and is a direct link between the worshipper and God. There is no hierarchical authority in Islam and there are no priests. Prayers are led by a learned person who knows the Qur'an and is generally chosen by the congregation.

The second pillar is prayer five times a day. These prayers are said at dawn (*salat al fajr*), mid-day (*salat al bohor*), late-afternoon (*salat al 'asar*), sunset (*salat al-maghrib*) and at nightfall (*salat al leela*). Their timings vary everyday in connection with the rising and setting of the sun. Prayers are made to pay respect to God and to give him thanks. These five prescribed prayers contain verses from the Qur'an, and are said in Arabic, the language of the Revelation. Personal supplications, however, can be offered in one's own language and at any time. Prior to praying, Muslims wash themselves

in order to be ritually purified in preparation for prayer. Muslims can pray anywhere, be it indoors, outdoors, or in another country, but they must face Kaaba in Mecca as they pray. They rise and prostrate themselves several times during the prayer. The number of times a worshipper rises and prostrates is different for each of the five prayers.

Stores and businesses are not expected to close during prayer time but the man assisting you may disappear for a short while, leaving you alone in his shop, or his assistant might help you and then take his turn to go to the mosque.

Prayer is very important to Emiratis, but prayer practices are not as extreme as they are reported to be in Saudi Arabia. There is no public criticism of people who choose not to pray. Most men do not get to the mosque for every prayer, but they do try to make it there at least once a day. Friday noon is the most important prayer time of the week and political speeches are given along with the usual religious messages. Women usually pray at home though there are mosques for women only. Other religions hold their usual main services on Friday and a smaller one on Sunday for those who can make it. Friday is the one day a week when everyone has the day off.

Oftentimes visitors to the Muslim world are struck by the centrality of prayer in daily life. Muslims are notified of prayer time by a call broadcast from loudspeakers at the top of mosques. There are plenty of mosques in the UAE so all can hear and heed the call.

A Translation Of The Call To Prayer (*Adan*)

God is Great. God is Great.

God is Great. God is Great.

I testify that there is none worthy of worship except God.

I testify that there is none worthy of worship except God.

I testify that Muhammad is the messenger of God.

I testify that Muhammad is the messenger of God.

Come to prayer! Come to prayer!

Come to success! Come to success!

God is Great! God is Great!

There is none worthy of worship except God.

It is unlikely you will see a beggar in the UAE, but if you do, you should give something even if it is only a few coins. If you do not have those, then say *"Allah yateek"*, meaning "May God give you." In so doing, you have at least given a blessing.

The third pillar is giving alms to the needy. Muslims are required to give a percentage of their goods or earnings to the welfare of the community and also to the poor. In the UAE, food is distributed once a week at palace gates to the needy who come for it. The principle of Islam behind alms-giving is that everything belongs to God, and therefore wealth is held by human beings in trust. The word *zakah* means both 'purification' and 'growth'. Our possessions are purified by setting aside a proportion for those in need and for the society in general. Like the pruning of plants, this cutting back balances and encourages new growth. Each Muslim calculates his or her own *zakah* individually. This involves the annual payment of a fortieth of one's capital, excluding such items as primary residence, car and professional tools.

The fourth pillar requires Muslims fast during Ramadan. A fasting Muslim takes neither food nor drink, not even water, between sunrise and sunset. Smoking is also prohibited during Ramadan as are sexual relations. Fasting causes the Muslim to know hunger and deprivation and many are humbled by the experience. This act of self-discipline is an expression of faith. Although fasting is beneficial to health, it is mainly a method of self-purification and self-restraint. By denying oneself worldly comforts, even for a short time, a fasting person focuses on his or her purpose in life by constantly being aware of the presence of God.

The fifth pillar requires Muslims perform a pilgrimage to Mecca at least once during their lifetime if it is not a financial hardship. Mecca is located in Saudi Arabia and is Islam's holiest city. Over two million people make the journey each year from every corner of the globe, providing a unique opportunity for those of different nations to meet one another. This pilgrimage is known as the *hajj* and is the height of religious experience for Muslims. The *hajj* is performed in the 12th month of the Islamic year. Muslims come to Mecca and carry out worship activities and rituals at different holy sites there over a period of six days. These activities and rituals end with the sacrificing of a sheep by those who can afford it. They share their feast with those who cannot. Pilgrims wear special clothes—simple garments that strip away distinctions of class and culture, so that all stand equal before God.

The rites of the *hajj* include going around the Ka'bah seven times, and going seven times between the hills of Safa and Marwa as Hagar (Abraham's wife) did during her search for water. The pilgrims later stand together on the wide plains of Arafat (a large expanse of desert outside Mecca) and join in prayer for God's forgiveness, in what is often thought to be a preview of the Day of Judgment. The close of the *hajj* is marked by a festival, the 'Id al Adha, which is celebrated with prayers and the exchange of gifts in Muslim communities everywhere. This and the 'Id al Fitr, a festive day celebrating the end of Ramadan, are the two holidays of the Islamic calendar.

Ramadan

Ramadan, the month of fasting, takes place during the ninth month of the Islamic calendar. Because of the difference between the Islamic calendar and the Gregorian one, Ramadan occurs about two weeks earlier every year. The name 'Ramadan' is taken from the name of this month, and the word itself derived from an Arabic word for intense heat, scorched ground, and shortness of rations. It is considered the most venerated and blessed month of the Islamic year because it is the time when God revealed the Qur'an to Prophet Muhammad. Muslims are supposed to focus on their spiritual growth and development during this month through increased prayer, meditation and observance of religious practices.

Ramadan is looked forward to with great anticipation. The month prior to Ramadan has a festive, holiday atmosphere to it. It is called Sha'ban, the time to make preparations. Emiratis and other Muslims redecorate their homes to prepare for visits from family, friends and neighbours. Many new clothes are made for the Emiratis by local tailors who work long, hard

Shops are open late during Ramadan to meet the schedule needs of people fasting. The *souks* hum with life and a walk through them will allow you to witness the holiday spirit during the night, when the temperature is cooler.

hours to complete the orders. It is a good idea to postpone trips to a tailor until after Ramadan if having a new outfit made. Emiratis purchase large amounts of goods such as pillows and carpets to sit on and mattresses for their many anticipated overnight guests. Large amounts of food are also purchased, especially staples. Emiratis keep plenty of snacks on hand; dates and nuts are particularly popular. All this shopping greatly eases the chore during Ramadan when people are too hungry to attend to it.

People also prepare for Ramadan during the month of Sha'ban by resolving conflicts they are having with others. They finish large projects and diminish their workload. This enables them to purify themselves and enter into the spirituality of Ramadan without distraction. Women have special preparations since they can anticipate being 'unclean' and therefore unable to participate in the fasting for part of Ramadan. This unclean time is a woman's menstrual period. She is prohibited from fasting as are pregnant women, those in poor health and young children. Children begin to fast (and to observe prayers) from puberty, although many start earlier. Women must make up the missed time either before or after Ramadan. Those in poor health must make up the missed time when they are able. People who travel should not fast and are also required to make up the missed time.

The most prominent event of the month of Ramadan is the daytime fasting (*sawm*) practised by most observant Muslims. Everyday during the month of Ramadan, Muslims around the world get up before dawn to eat the *suhoor* meal (the pre-dawn meal) and perform their *fajr* prayer. They break their fast when the fourth prayer of the day is due.

Many Emiratis attempt to read the entire Qur'an during the month of Ramadan. This does not leave them much time for other academic pursuits. Ramadan does not excuse a Muslim from his or her duties; however, in reality, in the UAE school and work hours are reduced and less is expected because people slow down mentally and physically from the effects of fasting as the month continues. Evening prayer services are held nightly and special hours are set aside for women. It is the one month of the year when women regularly attend the mosque.

Work hours are shorter during Ramadan than they are during the rest of the year. Working hours change so that most work is done in the early morning or late at night after the fast has been broken. The evening meal is called *iftar* and is often followed by a very late night or early morning second meal (breakfast) called *suhur*. The Ramadan schedule can be quite intrusive if you live in apartment housing that has shops on the bottom floors. Work may continue through the night in those shops and be closed during the day. There is not much you can do about the disturbance because Ramadan takes precedence over your needs. The schedule differences that occur also make it a less than ideal time to be a tourist in the UAE, unless the tour is for the purpose of experiencing and participating in Ramadan.

Ramadan Tip

During Ramadan, all residents and visitors are required to abide by restrictions imposed on Muslims. While you will not be expected to fast, it is illegal for you to be seen eating, drinking or smoking in public between sunrise and sunset. You should be careful even in the privacy of your own home not to eat or drink in front of a Muslim. It is very rude to tempt someone focused on improving their spirituality.

Fasting brings on somewhat of a religious fervour, or euphoria. People feel very close to God and in tune with their beliefs. In the 'Gulf playground' this results in less tolerance towards Western vices. All restaurants are closed until the evening prayer call is heard. Bars are closed for the month; instead, hotels open shop in their larger suites. Hotel rooms become temporary bars and non-Muslims enjoy modified drinking and dining gatherings during daylight hours. Due to greater observance of religious practice, deviations from the law are less tolerated during this month.

Tempers get shorter as the month and the fast progresses and your tolerance level may need to go up accordingly. Muslim scholars claim that the fast is beneficial in two ways. Physically the fast is supposed to cleanse the system.

Spiritually it is beneficial for gaining greater control and discipline over the body's needs. You may wish to try the fast yourself to enter into the spirit of the season and to gain deeper understanding of your hosts. The biggest challenge is depriving oneself of water particularly since Ramadan occurs in the summer months.

The spirit of Ramadan has gone a bit of the way of the spirit of Christmas in the West. Whereas what has already been said is technically accurate, Ramadan is also a big festival when people overindulge at night and often spend large amounts of money on lavish gifts and banquets.

The Holy Qur'an

The Qur'an contains the doctrines of Islam exactly as they were revealed to the Prophet Muhammad. These revelations took place over a 22-year period. They explain correct behaviour for almost every aspect of a Muslim's life in order to attain salvation on the final judgment day.

The Qur'an is mostly written in verse which is both cadenced and rhyming. Some of it is written in prose. Both lend themselves beautifully to recitation. In fact, the word 'Qur'an' means 'recitation'. Those who can recite the entire Qur'an are bestowed the title Hafiz and are highly respected for their ability. Education in the past consisted solely of reciting the Qur'an. Memorisation of Qur'anic passages continues, but it no longer forms the entire educational curriculum.

The poetic quality of recited passages is truly beautiful. Emiratis and other Arabs take the aesthetic beauty of the Qur'an as proof of its being given to man by God. Emiratis have special jewellery they wear around their necks or, for men, on their dagger belts for holding favourite Qur'anic verses. These were ornate silver compartments in the past, though now they are more likely to be made from gold. The older, tarnished and beaten-up jewellery can be found in the *souks* and make for popular souvenirs among tourists.

God revealed the Holy Qur'an to the Prophet Muhammad in Arabic. Arabic is thus taken as the language standard in all Arab countries. Arabs value the ability to read and write the standard. Dialects, as different as they can be from the standard, are not written and this has helped maintain a standard language across all Arab nations through time. Further, a translated version of the Qur'an may be used for study purposes, but not for prayer. So if you aspire to convert to Islam, it will be necessary for you to learn Arabic.

Strife Over Israel

Volumes have been written on this topic. Most accounts are biased in favour of one point of view or the other. This account is a simplified and brief one to give you an overview of the issue.

Thousands of years ago, the Jews were driven out of their homeland and became slaves in Egypt. God promised to release them from slavery and deliver them to the promised land, known as Israel, after wandering without a home for a long time (many, many generations). When the Jews finally arrived in the promised land, Israel was occupied by Palestinians who did not recognise the Jewish claim to their land. The two groups have been fighting over Israel ever since. It is currently occupied by both the Jews and the Palestinians.

Governments of various countries have sided with one group or the other. The Emiratis do not support the Jewish occupation of Israel. They deal with the issue by denying it. On maps given to you, purchased or found at travel agencies, you may see that Israel has been marked out with a black marker. The topic is often prohibited from discussion. Flights to Israel cannot be taken from or arranged in the UAE and if you have an Israeli stamp in your passport, get a clean passport as you will not be issued a visa otherwise. If you are Jewish but hold a passport from a country other than Israel, you may be able to enter the country because your name may not make your religion apparent to the immigration officials.

The US often has an advisory against travelling to Israel and other Arab countries. This means they will probably not offer you assistance within the country if you are in danger or trouble because of political strife. Conflict among the Arabs, while frequent, is usually verbal, hence the endless peace talks between the different nations. Actual combat only occurs when things get out of hand and and when they do, the combat is usually short-lived.

Other Religions

The UAE is considered one of the most liberal and broad-minded countries in the region in terms of governmental and societal attitudes toward allowing the practice of other faiths. A few of the faiths represented are Indian Orthodox, Coptic Orthodox, and Roman Catholic, each with their own church buildings. The UAE government generally follows a policy

A decorated Christmas tree standing near a mosque in Dubai bears witness to the level of religious tolerance displayed in the UAE.

of tolerance toward non-Muslim religions and, in practice, does not interfere very much with their religious activities. However, the government does prohibit non-Muslims from proselytising or distributing religious literature under penalty of criminal prosecution, imprisonment, or deportation, deeming such behaviour to be offensive to Islam.

Djinn

Emiratis have a pre-Islamic belief in the supernatural which has survived the centuries. *Djinn* are spirits which can be either good or bad. They look very much like people and can even take the form of people we know. They have lives of their own and a society underground from which they occasionally arise. They live in the desert and are reluctant to enter the city. The Emiratis' pre-Islamic belief in them serves the purpose of explaining anything they do not easily understand. Emiratis claim the *djinn* can help or hurt people. *Djinn* are mentioned in the Qur'an, which both provides people the greatest protection against them and lends them validity in the eyes of the Muslims.

Djinn are thought to appear most likely at dusk or dawn and people should be very careful at those times not to harm them by inadvertently stepping on them, riding over them or throwing something on them. The harmed *djinn* will repay the responsible party in kind. Of course, if one were dutifully at one's prayers, none of this would be a concern. Stories abound of encounters with *djinn*. You might be told one of these stories, but then again you might not because the Emiratis suspect you will not believe.

WOMEN IN THE UAE

One of the greatest misconceptions about women in the UAE is that they are repressed, without rights, and hidden from the public as women are in many other Arab countries. This could not be further from reality. With the Emiratis comprising only 20 per cent of their country's population, hiding the female half from public is simply not feasible. Emirati women are seen at all places and their main scarcity is in the numbers—they make up just 10 per cent or less of the entire population.

The government has ensured significant educational and work opportunities for women, going so far as to ground these rights into the UAE Constitution. The Constitution, in accordance with the precepts of Islam, guarantees social

justice for all its citizens. Women are accorded the same legal status as men, the same access to education, health care and social welfare. They are legally allowed to claim title and have the same right to practise professions as men. Equal pay for equal work is proscribed. Women are even appointed to the Federal National Council.

Challenges To Advancement

The challenge to change with regards to women has been the traditions of a patriarchal society. The UAE women understand this and have pushed for change and access to opportunity at a rate and in a cultural manner acceptable to Emirati society. For this reason, unprecedented change has gradually come to be accepted as the norm. UAE women have looked at models of female advancement in other nations and determined that what they see in the West is not the model they wish to follow, primarily because the question of who cares for the children is not satisfactorily answered when women choose to work.

A new law passed allows divorced or widowed national women who were married to non-UAE citizens to pass on their citizenship to their children. This law is significant as a means to increase the population of UAE citizens.

UAE Civil Service Law allows for extensive maternity leave and recent rules provide additional payments for children and housing just to be sure there is no gender-based discrimination among employees. Despite these improvements, women tend to stay home once they have children. Infanticide was made illegal and this largely increased the survival rate for female babies. The demise of the traditional family unit is also something Emirati women have sought to avoid, but divorce has emerged as an issue.

The Qur'an And Status Of Women

Before the Prophet Muhammad began preaching the teachings of Allah, women truly did hold a subordinate position in Arab society. Islam is mistakenly thought to have lowered the status of women when in fact it raised their status through granting them rights where they were previously denied.

Women no longer had to marry their cousins, but were allowed to marry any man who was a believer. The Qur'an states that a woman's dowry is to be given to her and not to her family. Thus, she may truly own her personal wealth. It became illegal for a man to divorce his wife on false charges, and extramarital affairs became equally as wrong and punishable for men as it had been for women. The right to divorce her husband through a petition to the Shari'ah Court after paying compensation or returning her dowry, while in draft form as of this writing, will come to pass and is considered a landmark for women's rights in the Arab

Emirati women display wealth through their jewellery. This woman can boast of a substantial dowry.

world. The court has established family guidance committees to provide a social support system for families to resolve their differences and help preserve the family unit through counselling and mediation. Divorce is a significant issue in Emirati society. The government encourages marriage between nationals by rewarding the newlyweds with a sum of money. This was abused, with nationals marrying each other and quickly filing for divorce only to remarry again, collecting the government dowry each time. Now a couple must be married two years before they can collect the money. The government discourages nationals from marrying foreigners by regularly printing reports of a high divorce rate in these mixed marriages.

Progress in the role and status of women following the advent of Islam was slow in the Gulf because of its isolation from much of the developed world until about the last 30 to 40 years. Men and women are considered to be equal in God's eyes. According to Emirati belief, people should be measured by their piousness and devotion to their religion rather than by their skin colour or gender. Thus, holding women in subordinate roles was due to traditional institutions and their resistance to change more than to Islam.

Wealth

Women have the right to own property. Women mainly acquire their wealth through inheritance. The Qur'an says a woman is entitled to inherit half as much as her male siblings. Even though this amount is half of what a man may inherit, it is 100 per cent more than during pre-Islamic times. A woman also acquires wealth in the form of gifts when she marries. These gifts are bestowed on her by the husband and his family and include many valuables, such as gold and precious jewels. In fact, UAE women store their wealth in the form of jewels and wear them every day without the least bit of self-consciousness.

Women have complete ownership of their wealth and they do not contribute to household expenditures. Men are expected to provide complete material welfare for the upkeep of the house, yet household purchasing decisions are usually made by the wives. Women who actually use their wealth to further grow it or enter into business have been few, but more role models are establishing themselves in the field of business and investment as time passes. For example, the UAE had more than 11,000 businesswomen managing investments worth more than US$ 4 billion in 2006. Often though women defer to the wishes or advice of close male relatives or do not do anything with their wealth at all. Some wealthy widows may hire an agent to conduct their business. This gives them freedom to do as they please through a male voice.

Responsibilities

Women uphold traditions and customs by practising them in the home and by passing them on to their children. They are encouraged in this respect through societal pressures. The behaviour of children reflects back upon the success of a woman in her role as a mother, and a husband's praise and admiration of her in this role come as welcome rewards. A wife manages affairs concerning the home and family. She directs decisions about education and marriage and provides her children with the emotional support they need. They depend on her for this support their whole lives.

A wife budgets all home expenses. This is more often a matter of deciding what to spend money on, rather than how far the budget will stretch. Where there is more than one wife, each is provided for equally and is in charge of her own children and affairs. It is common for a good relationship to exist among wives of the same husband and when this is the case, the women will share child care and household oversight.

The wife supervises the servants of which there can be many. Servants cook, drive their employers to school and the market, clean the house and take care of the children. Most households have at least one live-in servant; others have more servants than family members. Stories make the rounds among the Emiratis of children who are raised almost exclusively

When asking a young Emirati how many siblings they have, you may be asked for clarification as to whether you mean how many from their mother or how many from their father.

by servants and speak Tagalog or Hindi better than Arabic! There may be such cases but it is more likely the rumours have been embellished to encourage women to be more attentive mothers.

As for a wife's conjugal duties, they are not usually considered duties but rather privileges of marriage. Sex is encouraged within a marriage in this society. An Emirati's sex life is as normal or abnormal and varied as any. However, a couple's sex life is considered to be a very private matter and will never even be alluded to. In fact, enquiring about the health of a man's wife is a grave offence as it implies the woman is loose. None of this is to say the topic of sex is not discussed, it is and at length. Children learn all they ever need to know in the *majlis* where the women discuss the general topic quite descriptively without ever making reference to personal experience. Children are much discussed in the *majlis*—their characters, their physical features and their reputations, as mothers are seeking suitable mates for their own offspring and want to make the best possible marriage match for their children.

When it comes to marriage, most women in the UAE have the freedom to choose their husband. Parents influence the decision through recommending or putting forward their preference. The daughters may request to meet the prospective husband before agreeing to a marriage. Young people flirt discreetly by looks, exchanged notes, text messaging and online chatting. The Emiratis have had their share of scandal, illicit affairs and unwanted pregnancies but these are not acceptable and the repercussions are so great, from stoning, being outcast and having ruined reputations, that the behaviour is discouraged.

Finally, the wife is responsible for attending to guests. For male guests she is behind the scenes directing servants in the kitchen and making sure the feast is lavish enough and well-presented. With her female guests, her manners are impeccable because she herself has been taught well. She rises when anyone other than a servant or child enters a room, she says 'hello' and 'welcome' repeatedly and asks about her guests' comfort throughout a visit. She gives her guests the seat of honour and encourages them to eat endless amounts of food, while eating little herself. She is a confident and excellent hostess, remaining dignified and in good humour.

Juha

Storytelling is an effective way to pass on traditions and values. Stories of Mulla Nasrudin or Juha have been told for centuries and throughout the world. In the UAE, this character is known as Juha and stories about him are used to teach wit and wisdom to Emirati children. The Emiratis love good deeds and hate evil, and Juha stories teach children this difference as well. His stories are often comic tales with a hidden meaning or moral lesson.

A Story of Juha

A countryman who enjoyed hunting once visited Juha in the city and brought him a hare as a present. Juha took the hare to his wife, had her roast it in the way he most relished, and invited the hunter to stay and share it with him. Some days later a man knocked at Juha's gate. "Who is it?" he called. "A neighbour of your good friend the hunter, who brought you the hare the other day," the man shouted up. Juha asked him in and let him rest and set a meal before him most hospitably. Not long after this, another stranger in country clothes called on Juha. "Who are you?" asked Juha. "I am a friend of the neighbour of the hunter who gave you the hare." "Welcome, welcome," said Juha who led him inside. When the guest was comfortably seated, Juha placed in front of him a steaming bowl of hot water. "What is this?" asked the stranger. "This water was boiled in the very same pot as the hare that my good friend the hunter, whose neighbour you know, brought me," said Juha.

Passing Time

Emirati women devote hours attending to beauty, from applying henna to their hands and feet and visiting beauty salons, to having their nails manicured and their hair treated with oils. Until recently, exercise was not part of the beauty regime. In fact, movement was avoided whenever possible and not just because of the heat. Large, soft women are beautiful to the Emiratis. Heavy-set foreigners are often more comfortable in the Middle East in general because it is a place

An Emirati woman buying groceries at the local market.

where they can feel beautiful and desirable, an escape from the reed-thin ideal in other countries. However, great obesity falls outside the realm of desirability. It is not true that the size of a man's wife reflects his wealth. The number of wives, rather than size, is a more accurate indicator.

When not entertaining guests, studying, caring for children or primping, Emirati women are shopping. Endless hours are devoted to purchasing shoes and jewellery, and to visiting tailors for the purpose of having numerous dresses made. It is amazing what a good fit a tailor can achieve, never having taken measurements of the woman for whom he has made a dress. Shopping efforts are stepped up for special occasions such as Ramadan and weddings, when wardrobes must be entirely revamped. This seems a bit excessive when they only cover themselves in black scarves, but the Qur'an advises them to dress well albeit discreetly. Nor is their effort wasted. How well they dress reflects their status. The moment they arrive at a function, their veils are removed and their female relatives see them and form or reinforce already-formed opinions of them.

Not all Emirati women are lithe and graceful. Some look awkward in their lovely gowns as if they were wearing them for the first time. Not all the women are beautiful either. Some are shy while some are outgoing, and some are self-confident but others are not. There is as much variety in personality and appearance with them as there is in any culture. However, two characteristics that do abound are hospitality and virtue.

In Public

Emirati women are often escorted by a close male relative when in public. Some of them have trusted drivers to take them to specific destinations. These drivers may be servants who have been with the family for many years and have thus earned a loyalty and trust akin to that reserved for family members.

Women may be seen in pairs or groups at the shopping centres or with their children and maids in the market places, and they are also seen at work. In Al-Ain, women staff the new shopping centres and hold 30 per cent of all management positions, and outnumber the men in the UAE government sector. UAE women represent 40 per cent of the workforce in education, 35 per cent in the health sector and 20 per cent in social affairs. However, their overall share of the total labour force is under 30 per cent.

In the past, Emirati women did not eat in front of strangers. This practice has relaxed and women can choose between the public areas of restaurants or the private rooms, partitions and family rooms where single men are not allowed.

Naturally, foreign women are more likely to encounter Emirati women than foreign men are, and often there are Emirati men and women working in the same position, available to help those of their respective gender.

In Politics

In 1975 Sheikha Fatima bint Mubarak, the wife of the late Sheikh Zayad, led the establishment of the UAE Women's Federation, now called the General Women's Union (GWU), to pull all women's societies together under one umbrella. This organisation, funded by the government, has been instrumental in preserving the culture by bringing attention to issues concerning women, children and the family. It has also helped preserve the Emirati culture through programmes introducing traditional handicrafts, and providing education in health, religion and literacy.

The organisation has grown in stature and is often responsible for introducing new laws, conducting research pertaining to women and children and making recommendations to relevant government departments. The GWU has strong ties with Arab and international women's organisations, the United Nations, and non-governmental organisations (NGOs) or non-profits. Through their work these women are raising the debate of the advancement of women with a vocal assumption of gender equality.

UAE's First Woman Minister

Sheikha Lubna Al Qasimi was appointed Minister of Economy and Planning in November 2004. She is the first woman to hold a ministerial post in the UAE, and is a member of the ruling family of Sharjah. She also holds a Bachelor's Degree in Computer Science from California State University, Chico, and an Executive MBA from the American University of Sharjah.

The United Nations Development Programme (UNDP) indicated in its report on human resources for 2007–2008 that the UAE is ahead of the US, the UK, France, Canada, Greece, the Republic of Ireland, Japan and Poland with regards to women representation in the parliament. In 2006, women in the UAE's Federal National Council (FNC) represented 22.5 per cent of the total number of members of parliament.

At Work

The Arab world, as a whole, is currently witnessing one of the world's fastest growth rates in terms of developing human capital and this includes Arab women. Though UAE women have only had the opportunity to work for the past 15–20 years, they are beginning to make up a substantial percentage of the workforce. This has come about mainly through Emiratization, a policy encouraging the hiring of nationals. Women have worked primarily in education, health and government. However, they are making strides in less traditional female roles, as local oil companies are also employing them as geologists and engineers. Because there are so few UAE nationals, women are strongly encouraged to obtain a university degree and enter the workforce.

There are challenges to translating UAE women's remarkable accomplishments in education into employment. Relaxed social restrictions are helping and work is not seen as merely a source of income but as establishing personal identity. Thus in recent years women have been spreading across the entire civil service and now account for about 16 per cent of all Emirati employees, or approximately 65,000 women. The unemployment rate among national women at approximately 20 per cent is more than twice that of national men even though women college graduates greatly outnumber male college graduates. This has to do with the patriarchal society and traditional views that are slow to change. It is also because some companies restrict the numbers of females they employ, or that their education may not be relevant to the needs of a technologically challenging workplace.

A wonderful career option and a very popular one for Emirati women is IT because it can permit women to work from

As a visitor to the UAE you may encounter women working at the airport checking passports or at the Chamber of Commerce. Should you stay longer you are likely to encounter them in all government offices. Oftentimes there will be two or three women helping you together as there is safety in numbers.

home and may require minimum interaction with others. IT has begun to emerge in the country, and a large pool of educated women have pursued these careers. Women are running businesses and working in trade, maintenance, finance and investment, the arts, medicine, the army, police work, property management, manufacturing, restaurants, hotels and construction. Female role models are emerging in all fields.

Women are able to have greater access to high-level executive positions in the UAE than women in other countries since the country has a need for more Emirati leaders, and because women are less likely to interact with the public in these positions. Where strange men come and go, such as in banks and public offices, women may be provided a private room or a wall with a hole for which to speak and pass papers and money through. This was a common practice when women were first introduced to the workforce but is decreasing with the country's growth. Women are treated respectfully by customers and co-workers alike. At the hint of scandal or the diminishing of their reputation in any way, they are likely to be removed from the workforce by their families.

Working women earn equal pay and time off for equal hours worked. They are given maternity and parenting leave and are paid their salaries when they take leave.

A Muslim woman is required to mourn in complete seclusion for four months and ten days when her husband dies. The government has legislated her job be held for her and her salary be paid to her during this period in order to encourage her to remain in the workforce.

Women in the UAE realise how important it is to be financially independent and are motivated to work in order to advance their careers. Additionally, the Emiratis acknowledge the need to increase their national workforce and are trying to introduce their women to the workplace. Despite all the advances, gender inequality remains an issue. The hurdle they must overcome is bringing about societal acceptance and that is slow and often backsliding.

Women in University

An example of how introducing new customs to the society may work lies in education. In 1977, the UAE opened a university in Al-Ain, and a separate women's campus and facilities were provided for. The number of women attending the university remained at around a few hundred for years. These women were provided on-campus housing with an imposing wall around the campus and guards at the gates. They were restricted from coming and going just as they would be at home. Their parents felt comfortable enough with the situation to allow them to attend university, while society waited with disapproving frowns for the outcome of such a daring step. When young women graduated without scandal, a few more families allowed their daughters to attend. Enrolment has steadily increased ever since.

Higher education for women has become the norm and women are accepted at all the colleges and universities that now exist. The UAE University has remained segregated by choice and will likely remain one of the most traditional of the higher education institutions in this regard. However, many of the newer institutions integrate men and women in the classroom.

The most backward and conservative of Emirati Muslims see a woman's role as that of a domestic supervisor responsible for raising children and providing sexual pleasure. More forward thinkers believe women should be educated, allowed to work and trusted with decisions. They remember the days when people lived in small villages and women were seen in public and had social freedom because of the safe environment. The greatest concern of both the conservative and the liberal thinkers is the protection of a woman's virtue. By and large it is the women, who by setting excellent examples, reassure society and thus advance themselves.

The deep-rooted tradition of falconry continues up till today, as an Emirati man trains his falcon to hunt for prey in the desert of Al Ain, Abu Dhabi.

Rectangular wind towers can be seen at the corners of this building in the old Bastakiya district in Dubai. Wind towers were a common feature of houses here in the past, and they served to catch the breeze, ventilate the houses and keep the people cool.

Horse racing captures the imagination and excitement of the Emiratis unlike no other sport. They have built race tracks such as this one in Nad Al Sheba, and hold races that attract the international horse racing community. The ruling classes of the UAE all have stables with the best veterinarians, trainers and jockeys.

The Palm Jumeirah is the world's largest man-made island, a residential and tourism destination located in Dubai and created by Nakheel Properties. This project was conceived when the Ruler of Dubai desired to solve the problem of Dubai's beach shortage. He drew a sketch of a palm tree and realised its fronds would provide more beach frontage than a traditional circular island.

The Souk Madinat Jumeirah in Dubai is a lively and colourful marketplace where visitors can experience the atmosphere of the *souk* in air-conditioned walkways, and shop for traditional wares of the UAE.

FITTING IN WITH THE EMIRATIS

CHAPTER 4

'I and my brothers against my cousin;
I and my cousins against the stranger.'
—Bedouin saying

TRADITION AND HERITAGE

The Emiratis were a nomadic people. They lived in small family groups travelling from oasis to oasis (an underground spring providing a small amount of surface water and vegetation for shade). Their separateness from other people and the isolation of the desert instilled a sense of patience and physical endurance that enabled them to survive in their harsh climate. There were unwritten laws amongst the desert people that strengthened the group. These rules also made survival possible, and form the basis of many of the Emirati cultural values. Social beliefs and values are the slowest aspect of any culture to change. Therefore, while modernisation has affected the Emiratis to a great extent, the Bedouin values still guide their behaviour today.

Hospitality

Hospitality may be the single most important law of the desert. Without it, people travelling in the desert away from their groups would die. Even poor people are required to feed and shelter strangers and guests for an obligatory three days. The guest may leave after a few days without ever having stated his name or business because it is rude for the host to ask. Without this hospitality, an individual would not survive the desert nor encounters with other people once he left the family or tribe. Even a fugitive, a person shunned from their own tribe, or a person guilty of a crime against their host is taken in and treated as a guest of honour for the obligatory three days.

The guest is taken into the *majlis*, food is served in platters on the floor and eaten using only the right hand (don't expect utensils). The left hand is strictly for hygiene functions. Coffee, the main symbol of Arab hospitality, is ground in a brass mortar with a brass stick. The sound of brass striking brass signals to people nearby that a guest has arrived. People stop what they are doing and gather in the *majlis* to greet the guest.

Help In The Desert

Arab hospitality is prevalent even in a modern society and an Emirati will never leave you in need. An invitation for coffee will extend into dinner and perhaps an overnight stay as well. I came to rely on this hospitality when I drove long distances. My second-hand car broke down from time to time in the desert heat. The first Emirati to come by always stopped to help me. Once, I thought I had enough petrol to make it the 130 km home—I didn't. Within five minutes a car stopped and a *mutawa* (a religious leader) siphoned gas from his tank to mine as his two bodyguards watched. The *mutawa* could have made his bodyguards do the actual siphoning but helping me enhanced his honour and elevated his reputation in the eyes of others.

Great shows of hospitality are prevalent on special occasions such as weddings, funerals and the month of Ramadan. A host's honour, reputation and face all depend on the lavishness of the presentation, which represents how hospitable he is. Outdoing each other in displaying hospitality has, in some places, gotten out of hand. Weddings are the most frequent and obvious display. The hosts invite everyone they know (uninvited guests are also welcome), feed the guests and send them home with huge amounts of food, purchase the latest gown from London and proudly display the bride in all her splendour before the guests.

Modernisation has affected the availability of traditional and renowned Arabic hospitality in the UAE. Despite the desire by the government to Emiratize the country, nationals are largely absent from the hospitality industry. Business and leisure travellers want an authentic experience as they globetrot, yet if their sojourn is short they may never meet an Emirati. Even residents encounter urban homes with gates and closed doors which have replaced the open and inviting tents the Emiratis once lived in. Stay long enough, learn a little Arabic, get away from the big city centres and the experiences will come.

Generosity

One of the five pillars of Islam—giving alms to the poor—instructs Muslims to be generous. The wealthy give money and food to their poorer neighbours. Abu Dhabi donates as much as 30 per cent of its income a year to poorer Muslim countries. Abu Dhabi, the wealthiest of the emirates, also shares its wealth with the six other emirates in the form of funds for education, hospitals, road construction and other subsidies. You are very likely to hear stories proudly told of a past relation who was generous to the point of personal ruin. One common story is of a man who, upon seeing yet another stranger approaching, quickly slaughtered his last goat and rushed out to offer the newcomer what meagre amenities he had left.

Philanthropy is actively fostered. A 'Dubai Cares' five-week campaign to raise one billion *dirhams* (approximately US$ 270 million) was born out of Sheikh Mohammed's vision to help countries achieve one of the United Nations Millennium Development Goals of providing primary education to every child by 2015. This is one of many international initiatives by the Sheikh of Dubai in which his children are heavily involved. The Sheikh sends his children to other nations to study their needs and involves the public in achieving big fundraising goals. He is not alone. Her Highness Sheikha Fatima bin Mubarak of Abu Dhabi promotes walk-a-thons and other fundraisers to prevent such things as diabetes. There are also fundraisers for autism centres, breast cancer awareness and so on.

On an individual basis, Emiratis are financially generous. They give a portion of their income in the form of alms as one of the pillars of Islam. They are generous in friendship, frequently extending invitations to outings in parks and *wadis,* and they give gifts at every opportunity. It is rude to refuse their gifts and offers because a refusal does not allow them to carry out their good intention. In some situations, the Emirati will call a thing a 'gift' while the Westerner applies the term 'bribe'. It is a fine line and small wonder many Western countries have attempted to eliminate gift-giving in professional situations as have many businesses and organisations in the UAE.

Hidden Emotions

A saying goes, 'It is shameful for tears to fall, but tears in the eye are like pearls.' Emiratis experience the same range of emotions as other people, but it is shameful for them to show tears, sadness and anger. They are experts at putting on a 'poker face', giving a blank stare as they weigh and balance their thoughts before speaking. They do not trust people who do not look them directly in the eye and their own gaze becomes more steady the greater the depth of their emotion.

An Emirati will seemingly become more agreeable the less he or she agrees with you. A close look will reveal an almost imperceptible underlying stillness set in the jaw, and a blank stare in the eyes. Quickly review which of your words or actions caused offence and apologise. This will be greatly appreciated. You will almost always find an Emirati willing to negotiate conflicting views or desires, but a wall will come up if you must have your way and it will be fortified by your insistence.

Seeking Forgiveness

I claim cultural ignorance when I realise I have caused offence, and am always forgiven. Once, when explaining the word 'successor' to a group of students, I began, "Well, when your present ruler dies..." There was a collective intake of breath, still faces and faces that were quickly converting tears to stillness. I apologised profusely, told them I could see I had done something wrong, and found another way to define the word. Emiratis believe that referring to someone's future death wishes it upon them. Had I not already had my students' trust and respect, I might not have caught my students off guard and would have missed the brief glimpse of pain my words had caused. The incident, however, was forgotten as quickly and completely as it was forgiven

Tribal Relationships

The Bedouin function as a patriarchal society. Their loyalties are to their kin and are felt strongest towards their closest family members. Loyalties are less strong the less closely-related people are. In the past, extended families travelled together. All members of the group were able to trace their lineage to one common man. As these families grew in number, they joined other related family groups and formed a tribe. In force, they were able to protect themselves from the threat posed by other tribes.

Group cohesion was the key to the survival of these tribes, so absolute conformity to the values of the groups was demanded. Behaviour that lent itself to group cohesion was acceptable and good, while behaviour which did not was dishonourable. Group members who broke the group's code of ethics or in some way refused to conform brought shame to the group, and the group turned them out.

Peace within a tribal group was imperative. Aggression was not allowed because it could result in harm being inflicted on a group member, which in turn would diminish the strength of the group. Modern Emiratis are a very peaceful people. They consolidated seven tribes into one confederation, settled upon their internal boundaries and have lived peacefully together ever since. An Emirati's loyalties are to his family first, then to his tribe and then to the confederation.

Value Of Men To The Group

Men had to protect the group from other warring tribes. The more protection a group had, the stronger they were. Because men added immediate strength to the group, while women only had the potential to produce sons, men were more highly valued than women. When a boy was born, there was dancing, feasting and celebrating. However when a female child was born, little was done to mark the event. This value has practically disappeared with the need for all Emiratis to be active members of society.

To say the Emiratis were a warring people paints a bloody picture that is not entirely accurate. Death was avoided since the death of group members weakened the group. Tribal feuds took the form of raiding each other's herds. These raids provided more food and more cattle for the successful raiders and as a result, added strength to their group. A stronger tribe would not raid a weaker one since to do so would cause them shame. The goal was not to eliminate each other, but to gain strength and hence, power over other groups. This value plays out

Public Circumcision

One ritual that tested a man's bravery was the public group circumcision of 8–10-year-old boys just reaching puberty. Boys were circumcised at this age because they were able to withstand infection better than a newborn. They were expected not to cry out in pain while having their foreskin removed. Instead, they were expected to shout with joy. Nowadays circumcision is more frequently performed in hospitals one week after birth.

monetarily now with the united pursuit of commerce and peace that is necessary to achieve their great prosperity.

The need for protection of the herds led bravery to become a highly valued characteristic in the male Bedouin. The lack of bravery brought shame to the Bedouin and also to his family and tribe. Suppressing physical or facial expression in the face of physical or emotional pain was a sign of self-control and courage and was also highly valued.

A man who lived up to the ideals of the group was considered honourable. Such a man would be renowned for

Emirati father and son—the father is the head of the family and his status increases with age. Sons are valued as potential protectors of the group.

his hospitality and generosity. His blood was purely Arabic and he could proudly trace his ancestry all the way back to the Prophet Muhammad. He sired many sons and worked without undue labour, for example, tending flocks. He was a dignified man but quick to exact revenge when his honour was slighted. He bravely defended the group when called upon to do so and the women of his family were chaste, their hand in marriage a sought-after prize. Such a man was greatly admired and still embodies the ideal aspired to today.

Value Of Women To The Group

The value of women, as in so many cultures, lay in their ability to produce sons. The children a woman bore belonged to her husband. Since children, sons specifically, would add to the strength of the group, it was desirable for a woman to produce children in general and sons in particular. Emiratis thus value in-group marriage because it increases the number of people in a group.

The traditional family structure seems to break down in many societies as they modernise and this is also true in the UAE. Divorce is increasingly common, as is the practice of marrying people of another culture. Unable to stem the practice of foreign marriages, the government enacted laws

permitting citizenship to children as long as they were born to national women or national men.

The Emirati women are the flowers of the desert. They are placed on pedestals and treated as reverently as precious jewels. Subservient from a Western perspective and in dire need of protection from their own point of view, the women perpetuate their role in this male-dominated society in accordance with their cultural and religious beliefs. At the same time, they are making tremendous progress.

Concept Of Time

Many Western and modern Asian cultures could be considered slaves to time. They buy, save, keep, take, spend and use time in a host of ways. The Emiratis though have been less concerned with time. In the desert there is no sense of urgency or haste and no sense of future. The attitude is that tomorrow will come, yesterday was, so why be concerned with any time other than now? While the pace of activity in the country has picked up, missed deadlines are still often the norm and long-range planning remains problematic, resulting in projects that need to be redone.

The difference in conceptualising time is a cause of frustration for many expatriates. Deadlines are made and set as absolutes in the mind of the expatriate, but they may not be met. This causes the foreigner to hurry up, yet wait a lot. It can be quite disconcerting for the expatriate to say 'see you tomorrow' and hear '*insha'allah*' (God willing) in response. If these delays frustrate you, do not show your frustration, since becoming emotional or losing patience will result in a lengthier wait. If you anticipate delays from the start, you will save yourself much grief.

Contact with the West has forced the Emiratis to adjust to Western time concepts to some extent. Work schedules are set and time-tables are made. Even the official weekend has been changed from Thursday and Friday to Friday and Saturday. However, even if a store or office is scheduled to open at 4:00 pm it may not actually open until closer to 4:30 pm. Such things as the cycle of the moon can now be accurately determined with scientific instruments, yet

Ramadan begins only when a designated *mutawa* sights the new moon himself, not when the West predicts it will appear. Emiratis have made other concessions to time in keeping with Western conceptualisation. Planes usually take off and land when they are scheduled to and movies begin on time. These are superficial conveniences; in reality, time just does not matter so much. If something is not accomplished on Monday, it will be accomplished on Tuesday or Wednesday—*insha'allah*. Your disappointment may be met with the expression, '*mafi mooshcola*', meaning 'never mind, it doesn't matter'.

Courtesy

As in many cultures, you should never point the bottoms of your feet at another person. Give and receive items with your right hand. When entering a room say, '*assalam 'alaykum*' (peace be upon you) to which all present will respond, '*wa'alaykum salam*' (and upon you be peace). This will interrupt a business transaction, a conversation or a grammar lesson. Human relations are held to be of utmost importance, so the foreigner must learn to accept and participate in these interruptions.

Following the opening greeting, all men shake hands with the newcomer and touch the tips of their noses about three times before parting. The number of nose-touches reflects the depth of feeling the parties have for each other. Women kiss each other on the cheek—once on the right cheek and three to dozens of times on the left, again reflecting the parties' depth of pleasure at seeing each other. Men and women do not usually touch each other and since there are many Muslims from other Arab countries, wait for a hand to be extended to you in greeting when in mixed company.

After greeting, a series of questions may follow about the health of each other and each other's family. For example:

A: How are you? Fine?
B: *Al-Hamdulilah* (Thanks to God).
A: How is your family? Fine?
B: *Al-Hamdulilah*.
A: How is your brother?

B: *Al-Hamdulilah*. How are you? Fine?
A: *Al-Hamdulilah*.

Even when the Emiratis speak in English to a Westerner, they carry out this discourse. So while the language is English, the culture is Arabic. The first speaker answers his own question with 'Fine' since greetings and responses are always positive and since you are obviously there and healthy, the speaker knows the answer. I often find myself racing along trying to accomplish an inordinate number of tasks only to come up against this discourse. It is as if someone were asking me to stop and count my blessings.

Wasta

As personal relationships are so important to the Emiratis, it would follow that who you know is far more important than what you know. *Wasta* is the clout you have by virtue of who you are or who you know. *Wasta* opens doors, generates necessary official stamps and signatures and generally moves things along a little more quickly. Expatriates do not as a rule have *wasta*, but they may know someone with *wasta*, which is almost as good. Some large companies employ a man who has no specific job title but whose job it is to provide *wasta* to newcomers. This man knows the ins and outs of society and can make your settling in a lot easier.

> Westerners may earn *wasta* in some circles. For example, frequenting the same stores and businesses regularly, especially if they are small, will bring automatic discounts and better initial prices. The storekeepers will be genuinely happy to see you whether or not you buy anything, and you may come to feel the same way about them.

The importance of *wasta* cannot be emphasised enough and the more you have or are able to acquire it through building relationships, the further you will go and the more easily you will find getting your work done and your needs met.

Fatalism

The Emiratis do not believe they are in control of nature or the things that affect them or their future. Problems or lack of advancement at work are due to bad luck rather than anything the Emirati might or might not have done. This is not to say the Emiratis do not work for what they want; they do. However, if they do not achieve their goals, they do not blame themselves. Rather, they attribute their failure to God's will, and trust that God wished them to have or do something else. This religiously-based philosophy is much different to that of many of the guest cultures.

Many Westerners are practically addicted to accomplishment and self-advancement, and may see the Emiratis and others who believe in fatalism as lazy, while the Emiratis see their efforts to control and direct the future as futile or even worse, sinful. Of note, work is quite different in the UAE from that of many places to which Westerners are accustomed, in that it allows for an extraordinary amount of leisure time.

Death

When a person dies, the body is adorned as it would be in life and placed on its right side facing Mecca in a trench dug in a hole. The trench is blocked with pebbles and the hole is filled with sand.

The survivors do not wear cosmetics, oils, incense, perfume or jewellery. Friends and relatives bring food for the immediate family for three days and are in turn offered coffee (but not food) as a sign of renewed friendship.

Men seldom visit gravesites and women never do. There is no mourning period for a widower, but a widow is secluded for four months and ten days. If she looks at a man who is not part of her incest group during this time, she must immediately bathe in order to purify herself. Other relatives mourn for a much shorter amount of time and grief is hidden in public.

Grief Concealed

A student came to me after having missed a week of classes and said, "Miss, I am sorry for missing class, but my mother died last week." I was quite moved and told her I was sorry for her loss. She matter-of-factly thanked me without the least outward sign of sorrow and took her seat.

Loyalty And Lineage

Members of a family show loyalty to each other through subservience and obedience to the best interests of the group. Family groups are led by a respected male figure who leads, guides and advises the members with wisdom and faith. Each member is loyal to all the other family members, including the extended family. The greater the loyalty of the individuals, the more united a front the family presents. In return, the family protects its individual members.

A woman is always a member of her father's family. Even when she marries into another family, her loyalty is to the family she was born into. For this reason, she does not change her name when she marries. This patrilineal descent can work in a woman's favour. If a woman's husband or her husband's family mistreats her, she has her brothers and father at hand to rise up in her defence. When a woman's sons are old enough, they provide her with the support similar to what she received early in her marriage from her father and brothers.

A woman's children are members of her husband's family. In a divorce, older children are automatically awarded to the father, unless special provisions have been made in the marriage contract. Patrilineal descent hence strongly discourages marriage to members of other families or tribes. Women take strength and wealth in the form of children and inheritance away from their paternal families and add it to their husband's family when they marry someone outside the paternal family. A woman's offspring represent strength and quantity, but these belong to her husband. Her wealth passes to her children upon her death and thus, out of her father's family and into that of her husband. The ideal marriage then is one between the children of two brothers. Progeny of such a union can trace a common ancestor, and wealth and strength are retained by the family.

Honour

Individuals are loyal and responsible to the group they belong before themselves. An individual's behaviour reflects back on the group and can bring shame and dishonour, or glory and honour. Pressure to maintain a good standing within the group is strong enough to deter most people from behaving in ways that would exclude them from their group. In the past, people who were tossed out of the group had no choice but to wander around the desert. This meant almost certain death. Even if the wanderers came upon other groups, those groups would provide them with only the obligatory three days of hospitality, but not group membership.

When individuals did bring shame and dishonour to their group through their misconduct, the group had to restore its honour. The only way a group could do so was to punish the guilty individual. The greatest dishonour a group could experience was that brought about through the sexual misconduct of one of its female members. These rules still hold true today. Thus, every aspect of Emirati society, from segregation and veiling, to being escorted and homebound, offers women protection from the possible loss of their honour. Women, recognising the value of their virtue, see these practices as providing them with protection and while they are finding ways to participate publicly in society, they strive to keep their honour.

A man's honour is called *wijh*. When a man loses his honour his face is blackened. Honour belongs to a man through membership in a tribe. It requires him to defend what is his (his land, flock, women, and other possessions) and to respond to the demands placed on him by his family or the tribe.

A woman who commits adultery will be punished by her father and brothers on whom she has brought shame. Capital punishment, the sentence for adultery, is rarely meted, since four witnesses to the crime are required to carry out the punishment. Where four witnesses cannot be found, the woman will receive 100 lashes. The husband is responsible for seeking revenge on the woman's

A man's honour could be lost by his inability to keep and control his possessions, including his women. Thus, the women under his protection could affect his honour through their actions. A lack of modesty in dressing or behaviour such that the woman would arouse other men would bring shame to the man. This power women wield over a man's honour causes him to both respect and fear his women.

lover who has impinged on his property rights. Revenge is exacted by killing the wife's lover. However, the husband has not suffered the dishonour her family has because she is a member of her father's family, not her husband's. The woman's family may regain face by punishing her, but the woman's honour is lost and can never be regained.

Maintaining Honour

A woman's honour can be harmed rather easily through a tarnished reputation. A friend of mine attended the woman's half of a wedding celebration. She was in a tent with 15 young, unmarried Emirati women between the ages of about 16 and 25. They were dancing wildly to an upbeat modern Arabic tune, gyrating their hips passionately in an effort to outdo each other. At a word from one of the older girls watching at a flap in the tent, the girls dove for their discarded veils, covering their skin, every dazzling jewel and every last stitch of embroidery. Breathlessly they began conversing in hushed tones and giggles as five older women marched into the tent. The women stayed about half an hour, eyes darting about behind their *burkas*, sizing up each of the young women present. The talk continued in hushed tones after the women had gone but gradually grew livelier and the dancing began again.

This same scenario played itself out several times throughout the evening. My friend asked why the girls stopped dancing when the older women came in the room and was told the old women, essentially the matchmakers, would think they were loose and hence spoil their reputations. So the whole scenario was a challenge, as are the tame (by Western standards) sideways glances across the market- place and the daringly bared ankles. Too much of it, and word gets around.

Feet And Sitting Positions

Upon entering an Emirati home you should remove your shoes. Shoes are seldom worn in the house because the floor is highly utilised as living space. Emiratis spend much of their time on the floor sitting, resting, cooking, eating and caring for children. They believe sitting on the floor is good for resting a tired body. Resting is best accomplished on hard cushions because soft ones can cause the back to ache. The practice of sitting on the floor is *sunnah,* or in accordance with the Prophet Muhammad's customs. It is thought to demonstrate modesty and to be more directly in contact with nature. Some Emirati houses sport chairs, particularly

the wealthy, the upper class and those who frequently receive foreigners as guests.

There are three customary sitting positions. The first is the cross-legged position where the shins cross over each other and the knees rest on the floor. The second is with the legs bent and both knees pointed in one direction, one leg resting on top of the other. The third position is with one leg bent as in the previous two positions and the other leg drawn up, the knee pointing to the ceiling and the foot lying flat on the floor. Westerners are not typically comfortable in any of these positions for long and fidget back and forth, alternating between them much to the amusement of the Emiratis who can sit in a single position for a prolonged time.

Feet should not touch the food tray, nor should the bottoms of feet be pointed at another person. Emirati men and women cover their feet with the edges of their long clothing and you would probably feel more comfortable if you were able to do likewise. Protruding feet do stand out.

Work Ethic

Westerners often view the Emiratis as decadent and spoiled and have a whole host of negative feelings arising from a lack of understanding. Many Arabs are adverse to physical labour, particularly if it dirties their hands or makes them sweat. The Emiratis do not work with their hands (perhaps with the exception of the women doing handicraft). They view the doing of projects around the house as demeaning, and think that Western hobbies and pride in completed projects are quaint.

> The Emirati work ethic is unlike that of the Protestant work ethic prevalent in the West. They avoid work that requires the use of muscles, and do not engage in agricultural work, except that in research and management positions.

Indoor labour is preferable to outdoor labour, and office work is better yet. Some Emiratis see work as a curse and hold the acquisition of wealth through luck as the ideal. However, gambling is illegal (against Islamic law). While they do not believe in gambling, opportunities abound to win large cash prizes or cars from businesses trying to attract customers.

Earning favour in the eyes of someone important in order to advance one's work position is positively valued. Nepotism is also prevalent among the Emiratis. Westerners ridicule them for their 'hypocrisy' and nepotism, non-Gulf Arabs envy them, but the Emiratis themselves believe they are blessed by Allah and have their just rewards as predetermined by Him.

The further away from manual labour Emiratis get, the higher their status. In a country as wealthy as the UAE and where the wealth is controlled by less than a quarter of the population, the Emiratis never have to dirty their hands, as there is a legion of foreigners available to do their labour Many of the Emiratis are owners of businesses and real estate. These owners, called businessmen, may also hold government positions, from policeman to ruler. While keeping some of the values of the past and integrating them into a changed lifestyle, the modern Emiratis have also insulated themselves from the rest of the population by high walls, tinted windows and special privileges.

We might view the Emirati who chooses to continue the desert life as poor and the city dweller as rich. However, the Bedouin way of life is highly revered and even the city dweller lives by the values and beliefs of the Bedouin. Not all Emiratis are wealthy, have good family connections or carry traditions that are highly revered. Poor Emiratis are most likely to be encountered in the northern, less wealthy emirates. They make their living from fishing, shop keeping and trading. The well-educated among them work as teachers and researchers. Abu Dhabi provides the northern emirates with funds for infrastructure to be put in place, so that education and health care are provided for. While these Emiratis are less likely to live in palaces, their basic needs are met.

Manners

You should always be polite with the Emiratis. Most of them treat expatriates very well. If you anger them (thankfully this is difficult to do) there can be repercussions, especially if the Emirati is highly placed. Conversely, if you build relationships and earn *wasta*, an Emirati can help you out in a bind. Young Emirati men can be annoying. Some of them are full of their own status yet lack the grace to treat others with dignity. They hoot and holler at women from their car windows, push ahead in lines, park their cars anywhere they please (for example, behind your parked car at the supermarket) and generally behave like the typical, rowdy young men you would encounter in most countries.

Most of their less desirable behaviour occurs when they are in their four-wheel-drive vehicles, Mercedes Benzes and BMWs. The anonymity of their vehicles gives them license to forget the values they were taught, just as it does for young people anywhere. If possible, say '*haram*' (forbidden) and the rules they learned in the *majlis* should kick in and change their poor manners. The government attempts to curtail poor behaviour by arresting offenders and publishing their photographs in the newspapers to embarrass them into behaving properly.

POINT OF DISCUSSION OR TABOO TOPIC?

Virtually all Emiratis are Sunni Muslim, and so is much of the rest of the population. Muslims pray five times a day and tend to be conscious of the teachings of the Qur'an between these times.

Putting harmful things into the body is against Muslim teachings. Drugs and alcohol are topics to avoid or to treat with care when questioned by an Emirati. Religion, politics and sex are also sensitive topics because the foreigner's view is usually different and more liberal than an Emirati's. If you do not feel you can politely listen to their views without comment, you might be better off indicating you are uncomfortable discussing the topics. This should prevent further attempts to engage you in a taboo discussion because the last thing an Emirati wants to do is make you feel uncomfortable.

It is acceptable to say positive things, but not acceptable to be negative or critical, and it is particularly taboo to criticise the government.

There are numerous acceptable topics of discussion. First and foremost is the topic of family. Enquiring about family will please an Emirati, though if you are speaking to a man, refrain from enquiring about the women in his family. This is bad manners because it implies that his women are loose.

Food is a safe topic. An Emirati will be happy to describe the kind of food he or she eats and how it is prepared. Don't be surprised if you are then brought a favourite dish. The Emiratis burn incense and blend perfumes endlessly. The

musky smells are a delightful part of daily life. An Emirati will like being questioned about their special or favourite blend of perfume.

Medicine is another topic that will keep a conversation going. Emiratis have concocted family medicines that have been passed from generation to generation. They are able to tell you about many different natural medicines and they have numerous true stories about curing people. If you exhaust these topics, do not worry—Emiratis are also comfortable with silence.

Opinions

Critical thinking and opinions are valued among people who value individualism. Group-oriented people on the other hand think not in terms of themselves but in terms of the good of the group. This group relies on the Qur'an to inform their opinions and guide their behaviour. Critical thinking and problem-solving abilities are not well-developed when all answers are found in a book. You may thus be disappointed by some of the answers you are given to intentionally thought-provoking questions, since average young Emiratis all seem to produce the same answers. It can sound like you are being given a lot of party propaganda. Critical thinking and problem-solving skills are now being introduced intentionally into school curriculums. Unfortunately, the content can be extremely censored and the process is slow.

While foreign media such as Star TV, CNN and the BBC are available in their uncensored form to the Emiratis and may spark curiosity in some, they instead encourage fundamentalism in others.

ALTERNATIVE LIFESTYLES
Homosexuality

Emiratis generally regard homosexuality as a deviant behaviour—immoral, changeable, chosen, abnormal and unnatural. Sexual relations outside of a traditional, heterosexual marriage is a crime in the UAE. It is punishable with jail time, fines, deportation, and the death penalty. The death penalty is seldom invoked as the UAE generally bows to international pressure against its use. If it is indeed used, it is minimally publicised.

Much research on the percentage of a population that is gay has been done over the past 50 years. These studies cite a low of less than 1 per cent to a high of 10 per cent for any given population and statistics are generally lower for women than for men. Which statistics are used depend on a person's agenda, so those advocating for gay and lesbian rights will cite the higher statistics and those wishing to explain it away as an anomaly will quote the low figure.

It is impossible to say what percentage of the population in the UAE is homosexual but most certainly the population does exist and may in fact be quite high because of the disproportionate number of men over women in the country.

In late 2005, 26 men were arrested in Abu Dhabi at what was thought to be a gay wedding. The 26 were from a variety of nationalities including Emirati. The incident gained national attention as it was believed the men were treated with hormones while in custody. This was soundly denied. Whether or not it was true, it does highlight the belief commonly held in the UAE that being homosexual is voluntary and can be corrected. Such behaviour is against Islam. The Emiratis believe children will not be prone to it if they follow virtuous behaviour and abandon vice.

The Internet has greatly enabled conversation on the subject and facilitated people meeting each other. It follows that part of the blame for having more homosexuals in the Arab world is therefore the fault of the West and the changes in technology introduced. Homosexuals would do well to exercise discretion in the UAE and be advised that gay and lesbian Internet sites are monitored, tracked and blocked.

SETTLING DOWN IN THE UAE

CHAPTER 5

'Things are not good and not bad, they are just different.'
—Author's mantra

ENTRY

Visas are not required for stays between 30 and 60 days. All guests staying to work beyond 60 days require a residency visa, though extensions of up to 90 days may be requested. In addition, an AIDS test is required for work or residence permits, and testing must be performed after arrival. New residents are usually only tested the one time.

Though not accepted, having an AIDS test conducted prior to departure to compare with the one you will receive when you arrive may help you get a second test in case of a false positive, and if you are going to be sent home, it will help you get the flight home paid for since you can demonstrate you did not have it when you departed. You will not be allowed to stay if you test positive for HIV or AIDS. A mandatory test for Severe Acute Respiratory Syndrome (SARS) and other infectious diseases is also required for a residency visa.

Required documents for a residency visa:

- Original and valid passport
- Letter of invitation from sponsoring company in the UAE
- Copy of the host's residency permit in the UAE
- Copy of the host's passport
- Two completed application forms
- Two passport photos
- Self-addressed stamped envelope

You are required to pay a fee. The Consul at the Embassy will decide how long you may stay. Carry plenty of passport photographs, as they are required for all official documents you will need when you first arrive.

The UAE has made visiting the country easy for citizens of many countries. Nationals of the UK, US, Australia, Canada, New Zealand, Japan and most EU countries are required to have a passport to visit the UAE. Passports must be valid for at least six months from the arrival date, and return or onward tickets are required. The visa is actually stamped in the passport upon arrival. Rules regarding who may enter the country and for what length of time are constantly evolving and it is best to check your local embassy for requirements according to your citizenship.

Entering With A Child

In an effort to prevent international child abduction, many governments have initiated procedures at entry and exit points. These often include requiring documentary evidence of the relationship between the child and an accompanying adult, and when the child's parent or legal guardian is not travelling with the child, permission from the parent for that adult to accompany the child is necessary. Having such documentation on hand, even if not required, may facilitate entry and departure.

The airports in Abu Dhabi and Dubai are crowded with people entering the country. Passport control is run by Emiratis who will stamp your passport. You may get in line according to your country of citizenship. Baggage is then picked up and you proceed to customs. Your bags should have been screened by the time you are through passport control and at the baggage carousel.

If you have been sponsored by an employer, they will communicate with you plans about your arrival. If it is a hotel that has sponsored you, there should be a shuttle for you to take to your destination. There are now six international airports (Abu Dhabi, Dubai, Sharjah, Ras Al Khaimah, Fujairah and Al-Ain), but you are most likely to arrive from abroad into Dubai or Abu Dhabi. Those with GCC passports may enter and exit the country without a visa.

Employees may find it difficult to change companies once they are working in the country because the law requires they leave the country for six months before being permitted to change companies and re-enter. People who opt to remain illegally may have their photograph published in the newspapers as a warning to other employers not to hire them. If you hold a residency visa, you may enter and exit the country without obtaining permits or stamps. However, some employers, particularly those with government affiliation, require you to obtain their permission to exit and re-enter the country. Failure to do so can be justifiable cause for your dismissal and deportation.

If your passport bears an Israeli stamp, you will not be permitted to enter the UAE. You can exchange a passport bearing an Israeli stamp for a 'clean' one before applying for a visa. This problem may crop up in other Islamic countries as well. To avoid it altogether, you can request officials in Israel give you your stamp on a separate piece of paper and not put it in your passport at all. It is not possible to book a flight to Israel by any route from the UAE.

Israel Blackout

Israel is censored out of many aspects of life in the UAE. Movies featuring Jewish actors, producers and directors such as Yul Brynner and Barbara Streisand are not usually available. World maps on the walls of travel agencies sport black ink where Israel should be and Jewish people are not allowed in the country.

At some point as you are trying to enter the country, an Emirati may likely step ahead of you, even if you are a woman. Lines are a Western concept, though they do exist in the UAE. Emiratis are not governed by the equality of first come, first served that most know, but by gender and nationality. Female nationals come first, then all other women, then national men and finally all other men.

Free Of Charge

While many items and services in the UAE are exorbitant, many other things are surprisingly free of charge. As of this writing, there is no airport tax; you will not pay for the cart you use to get your bags out of baggage claim; and customs will not charge you for any of the electronics you bring in. Most importantly though, Dubai's port is duty free. At other points of entry, import tax officially runs between 4 per cent and 20 per cent. However, as with many economic regulations imposed at an international level (such as copyright laws), they are not uniformly applied in practice. Over half of the goods that go in and out of the UAE do so duty free. Thus, goods pour in and out of the country at a terrific rate. Electronics, 22-carat gold and handmade carpets can be picked up in Dubai's markets for very reasonable prices.

CULTURE SHOCK
What Is Culture Shock?

Culture shock is what afflicts people who spend prolonged periods of time in another country. It pertains to how people cope with the stress caused by the newness of the environment, culture and people. The stress can feel like an illness and can cause physical problems such as allergies, backaches and headaches, or interrupt the normal digestive processes. It can bring on emotional stress expressed through unexpected and inexplicable tears or vehemently expressed anger over minor offences. It can also unsettle a person

intellectually to the point where they don't know who to trust and can't distinguish between reality and the fabrications of their imagination. People who are already under some emotional stress will feel the effects of

Culture shock is a stage of development one goes through in adapting to a new culture. It does not begin or end at specific times, nor is it brought on by individual and isolated incidents. It may recur in smaller doses throughout your stay.

culture shock much more severely than those who are not.

Culture shock happens to everybody to some degree or another. Even people who have experienced it before must go through it again in a new country and culture. You are hardly aware of the stress and changes you've been through until you watch other newcomers go through it and remember your own similar experience and feelings in those situations, and how much more comfortable you feel with the passage of time. Knowing what to expect can help, but it cannot prevent it.

Three Stages

In adapting to a new culture, one goes through three stages. An individual enters and exits these stages repeatedly but tends to fall within one of the three at any given time. The initial stage is one of euphoria in which everything about the culture and the overseas experience is new and wonderful. The newcomer then progresses to the shock stage in which they are angry and negative about the host culture and country. The final stage is one of acceptance. The developing newcomer adjusts to the culture and learns to operate comfortably within it.

Culture shock happens because of the human condition of expecting others to behave, think and feel as we do. Newcomers to a culture experience a constant barrage of conflicting behaviours. They are making sense of their daily lives according to the way their home culture organised life. When they must act or react in situations in the new culture, they will do so according to the rules of their own, or at least until they learn new ways of behaving. Their behaviour may not be appropriate in the new environment, causing them to be misunderstood, cause offence or be offended.

Newly-arrived expatriates must learn the new ways of behaving and change some of their behaviours, thoughts and emotions in order to cope in the new environment. Frequent encounters resulting in misunderstandings cause newcomers to feel anxious, confused, irritated and helpless. They may experience moments of depression and choose to withdraw from the world around them. They may feel extremely homesick and join other expatriates in drowning their feelings in alcohol and making disparaging remarks about the host culture. They may even develop paranoid thinking that people are watching every move they make. The more you insist on your view and your way, and the less tolerance you have in a situation, the more frustrating it will be for you. Anger, outrage and frustration are normal reactions. However, the Emiratis are outwardly gentle people who believe it is shameful to show rage. People around you will be amazed and embarrassed if you lose your temper. Aim for humour to diffuse the tension, or take a few deep breaths.

Culture Shock In The UAE

Descriptions of culture shock assume it is just one culture to which you are adjusting. The UAE is unique in that a single culture to adjust and settle into does not exist. It would appear that one has many choices of culture with which to mix. Choices are somewhat restricted by gender, language and social status. Outside of the expatriate group, men and women do not tend to mix socially—it is against the rules and norms of the society. Language can be a limitation. English and Arabic are widely spoken but there are also many who only speak Urdu or Hindi (or German, Chinese or Italian!).

If you choose to flout class boundaries and befriend a labourer who does have a reasonable command of English, he may misunderstand your overtures, make erroneous assumptions about you and your motives and behave in ways likely to cause you offence.

During the honeymoon stage you will find the sand dunes beautiful, the parties fun, the Arab women, hidden behind their veils, mysterious; and the markets humming with life and delicious smells. About four to six months after you arrive, the sand dunes all look the same as those you keep sweeping out from under the beds and corners of the rooms. The same people are at all the parties you attend, complaining about the same things. Constantly negotiating prices with people is more trouble than it is worth.

Expatriate behaviours may seem familiar. Almost everyone speaks English fluently. They enjoy the same activities, use the same modern conveniences and products, and have similar tastes in dress, music and so on. They are from many different cultures though, each making sense of and organising life according to a different set of rules. The most obvious difference is linguistic. Each group uses slightly different vocabulary and speaks with a slightly different accent. These differences form the basis of many interesting and humorous discussions.

Most Western newcomers stick to what is available and familiar—other Westerners. This requires its own adjustment. There are differences among the Westerners that are not so obvious. The independent American soon tires of her Spanish friend's constant presence. The distant Brit is offended by his Egyptian friend's inquisitive, personal questions. The Australian is surprised to find that discussing different viewpoints is taken as arguing and has been taken personally. The Scotsman tires of adjusting his accent to be comprehensible to other native English speakers. Almost everyone grows tired of being ridiculed for every stereotype particular to their country. They find themselves alternately representing and defending their home country. Laughter is a good antidote. So is education. Even altering one person's misconceptions or generalisations of your culture can feel rewarding. Watch, listen and learn about the interesting people around you. With a constant variety of cultural contact, it is impossible to adjust and settle into one culture. Thus, people form friendships with those they have most in common with. These are people from their home country, people they work

Support From Friends

Positive, upbeat friends will help you adjust. You need same-gender friends to give you respectability and to help you weather the inevitable gossip. This same gender group may also be your reality anchor, much as a family is for its members.

with, people in the same profession or teammates from the sport in which they are participating.

Handling Gossip

Gossip is rampant. It goes hand in hand with boredom. You will find yourself the focus of gossip from time to time with or without cause. Stories are sometimes embellished. In the face of so many ways of acting, thinking and feeling, rules and boundaries vary and the truth can be pretty amazing on its own. Ignore the gossip and fight the boredom by engaging in activities that teach you something new. The more you can learn about the Emiratis, the more interesting life will be for you. This may involve learning how to apply henna, speak Arabic or belly dance; studying about the archaeology and geology of the country, or learning about Islam.

GETTING AROUND
Directions

The use of street names and numbers is catching on, though oftentimes directions are given by landmark. With so many new buildings, many of them very tall and unique in some way, this method of direction giving is easy even for the newcomer. It helps too to have the coast as a reference point in much of the country.

Where's That Place?
Outside of the cities, there may be fewer signs, and directions become increasingly creative:

"Turn right at the coffee pot roundabout; go through the second roundabout; after 2.2 km you will come to a short bush in front of a camel crossing sign, turn right ..."

In the blinding white desert expanse the smallest sign of civilisation or life takes on relevance. In the cities landmarks such as roundabouts and mosques are prevalent and are used in giving directions.

Abu Dhabi is laid out in a grid with street names and buildings marked. Dubai's construction has been ongoing for several decades and directions such as, "Do you know where the old trade centre road used to be? No? Okay, how about the road that used to...?" are common.

Dubai has lessened much of the confusion with named neighbourhoods and districts, and with the advent of the metro system making a direct line through the city, traffic, transportation and directions will improve dramatically.

In many countries people on the street do not want to refuse you help, so if asking a stranger for directions, gauge their confidence in answering you. Even if they do not know where to send you, they may give you an answer rather than be so rude as to deny you help. This could set you off in the wrong way.

Taxis

Taxis are numerous and inexpensive, making them a great alternative to owning a car. In Dubai there are five different taxi companies and almost all taxis are now metered. The fare in 2007 started at 3 *dirhams* (dhs), or just under US$ 1, and costs 1.25 dhs per kilometre. Taxis to and from the airport are more expensive, with the meter starting at 25 dhs. If by chance you get in one of the few remaining taxis without a meter, negotiate the cost of your journey before it begins. Know your destination and how much it should cost to get there. Have your money ready to give to the driver when he stops. Tipping is appreciated. People who work in the service industry often send their salaries home and depend on their tips to pay for their living expenses. Taxi drivers will work until they have made enough in tips to survive, which is about 50–60 dhs a day, and this can make for long hours.

Everyone who takes a taxi, male or female, young or old, has a bad experience at some point. There are some precautions you can take in order to avoid having too many of them: sit in the back seat; do not make eye contact with the driver; remind him to turn on his meter if he has forgotten to do so; limit your conversation; be polite but firm in communicating your destination and no more; and speak with authority as though you know where you are going and the best route for the driver to take, even if you do not. If the driver does not appear to know where he is going, get out and take another taxi.

It is less safe for women to take taxis at night, especially outside of city limits—if at all possible, do not do it. As a woman, I follow these rules stringently when I am alone but I like to engage the drivers in conversation if I am travelling with another person. Taxi drivers offer a perspective on life in the UAE and have insight and access to parts of the culture that I don't.

Driving

Sponsors may offer their employees interest-free loans for the purchase of a vehicle or may even provide their foreign employees with vehicles, if the job requires the employee to travel from one site to another during a workday. A car will suffice for getting around since the surface roads are in excellent condition. Many people prefer four-wheel-drive vehicles for camping and recreation. Many vehicles in the UAE are white in colour. White reflects the sunlight so people think their cars will be cooler, but when it is 52°C (125°F), shade is the only thing that is going to make a difference to how hot or cool your car is. It is necessary to wash your car regularly and it is a good idea to rust-proof the vehicle. Car-washing stations are numerous, as are the labourers who will wash them everyday for very little.

One of the more unusual sights you may see on the road in the UAE.

Fuel for the car is cheap because it is subsidised by the government. You will not have any difficulties finding gas stations, but they may be closed at night so plan ahead for a trip with a full tank of gas. Cars are driven on the right side of the road and traffic is usually not bad anywhere except in the city of Dubai, between Dubai and Sharjah, and at certain times of the day in Abu Dhabi. Dubai is working very quickly on solving its traffic problems. Its rail system is expected to open in 2009 and should reduce traffic by as much as one-third. Widening roads and expanding bridges are also helping to ease congestion. Roundabouts are everywhere and are intended to cause drivers to slow down, but these have questionable effect. Roundabouts are built with less frequency now because with no clear signals, everyone tries to go forward at once and this causes traffic jams and slow-downs at busy intersections.

Licenses

International driving licenses are not recognised. Obtaining a license is fairly simple for many license holders who simply complete forms, have a valid driver's license from their home country and a residence visa, and provide the department of vehicle licensing with their passport and photographs. A license is then issued to the applicant for 100 dhs. Those not on a list of preferred countries also need a letter from their Embassy or Consulate confirming the validity of a license issued from that country. The list changes with more countries added all the time so check with the licensing authority. If the license is not in English or Arabic, it will need to be translated at the Embassy or Consulate.

You must always carry your license and registration with you when you drive. Police will stop traffic from time to time to check for licenses and registration. Sometimes they are looking for someone who is wanted for a serious crime. If you cannot produce your license and registration, your car will be impounded for 24 hours. You may have it back by producing your documents and paying the fines and impounding fees. You must also have third party insurance. This is calculated according to the year and model of your car.

Traffic Accidents

If you are ever involved in an accident you may move your car to the side of the road, but stay at the scene. Leaving the scene of an accident is illegal. The police will decide who is at fault and what property damage needs to be reimbursed. When you have paid your fines and fees, you will be given a letter from the police giving you permission to have your car repaired. Repair shops will not touch your vehicle without this permission. It is illegal for them to do so and could result in the closure of their business and deportation for both them and you.

Driving can be intimidating partly because driving laws and speed limits are not uniformly enforced and partly because there is so much traffic. Accidents are frequent, particularly in the congested downtown areas and fault is often split between drivers if the policemen can't decide who should be charged or if an Emirati is involved. Because of the frequency of accidents, one may wish to drive a large, new vehicle such as a four-wheel-drive. In addition to being safer, it is useful in the terrain outside of the larger cities. Women drivers are common. Some Emirati women have licenses but many also have their own drivers. So, while some of them can drive, they are not often seen at the wheel themselves.

Many expatriates choose to drive. My single, Western male friend chose to buy a car because not having one hampered his dating activities. Others choose not to drive because it is the likeliest cause of trouble and taxis are a viable alternative.

If you are in an accident and someone is hurt, the hurt person goes to the hospital and the unhurt person goes to jail regardless of who is at fault. If an accident results in death, the person who caused the accident must pay compensation for the death—this is called *dihhya* and is equivalent to about US$ 40,000. Insurance companies may refuse to pay, even when appropriate coverage is carried.

Outside of the big cities you will encounter livestock on the roads (or off roads). If you hit an animal, you are responsible for reimbursing the owner for the value of the animal. Camels can easily cost US$ 10,000. Stories are told of Bedouin letting their older camels roam near the freeways so they will be hit and the Bedouin reimbursed. More and

An accident with a camel is often fatal for both the camel and the occupants of the car because on impact, the camel's legs are hit out from under it and its body lands on the cab of the car, crushing the car and its occupants with its weight.

more fences are in place to keep livestock off the roads and it is hoped the laws will change so the owner is fined for allowing the animal to stray onto the freeway.

Prison Stay—An Account

The UAE ceases to be a benevolent place when a person commits what the government considers to be a serious infraction, knowingly or otherwise. For example, writing a check with insufficient funds, consuming or possessing alcoholic beverages in the wrong place, or living with someone of the opposite sex without the benefit of matrimony can land people in jail. In my case, it was a traffic accident.

On a fateful sunny October afternoon while returning to work, a pedestrian suddenly jumped in front of me. I swerved and missed him but then he jumped in front of me a second time and though I tried, I could not avoid hitting him with my front fender. He was thrown into the air and landed on my windshield. We were both taken to the emergency room. He was badly injured and spent more than two months in the hospital eventually recovering from his injuries. After negotiating a generous cash settlement with my insurance company, he returned to his home country of Syria as wealthy as he could ever hope to become. My injured hand was sewn and I was put in jail.

I shared a cellblock with 200 men in an area designed to hold no more than 60. My 'bed' was a wool blanket on the concrete floor, meals were served in large communal platters, utensils were not provided. According to law I was required to stay in jail for the amount of time it took the pedestrian to fully recover and leave the hospital. The family of the injured party could have agreed to my release earlier but did not. Nor did the courts move quickly and my time stretched to four months.

I was as comfortable as a person could be sharing so little space with so many men. My biggest challenge was boredom. I filled the time reading the same few books over and over again, visiting with my cellmates and playing an occasional betting game. Upon a fellow prisoner's release we would vie for their blanket and any clothes that might be in better shape than those we had. After three court appearances, a fine, and a sentence of 46 days, which I'd already served, I was released. My crime did not result in deportation and there was very little stigma around my having served in prison. I returned to work and life as I had known it for over a dozen years.

– Anonymous

Drinking And Driving

A lot of alcohol is consumed in the UAE. Westerners may obtain licenses to purchase alcohol. The license allows them to both purchase and transport alcohol to their homes only. Possession of alcohol when not in transit from the liquor store will result in a person's arrest if caught. An Italian acquaintance of mine borrowed a car and had an accident while driving it. An unopened bottle of whiskey (not his) was found in the back of the car and he went to jail.

If caught drinking and driving, you will go to jail. If you are in an accident and you have been drinking, you are in a lot of trouble. If no one has been injured, some consider it wise to walk away and then claim ignorance of the law when you do come back in a dead-sober state to take responsibility. You may at least avoid the lashings and prison stay. Many people drive home after a night out, but smelling alcohol on your breath is all that is required for a policeman to put you in jail. It is simply not a good policy to drink and drive in the UAE. Many, many more people drive without incident than have experiences like these. Nevertheless, they are emphasised here because the severity of repercussions is more than what many Westerners expect and it is easy to think this will not happen to them.

Other Transport Modes

Minibuses operate between all major cities in the emirates. They leave every 15 to 20 minutes or when they fill up. They have fixed fares. These buses can be quite full and so the front seats are reserved for women in an effort to culturally accommodate everyone. Noise from the engines may prevent conversation and the hard seats make long trips most uncomfortable. The four major cities have bus services with regular lines.

Visitors may rent cars. The telephone books are half in English and half in Arabic. Consult the yellow pages when you are interested in such things as car rentals but do not wish to pay hotel rates. Hotels can meet your every need, but they also charge much higher prices for their efforts than businesses not located in hotels. Travel agents can help you both within and outside the country, and all travel specific needs can be arranged online.

Walking And Cycling

Walking is almost impossible. When you are outdoors during the summer months, you do not even have to move to be drenched in sweat. Besides the unbearable heat, city blocks are long and cities are very spread out. Men may be able to do a little more walking than women, who will often be harassed by passing drivers. Cycling is not a transportation option for most people. Very few labourers cycle and an even fewer number of expatriates who are cycling enthusiasts have good options for riding. Cycling is dangerous because car drivers do not have much respect for those on foot or on a bicycle. Cars own the roads and where there are no roads, there is only sand.

The Eve Teasers

Men who harass women are called 'Eve teasers'. They are arrested and their photographs published in the papers to humiliate them and discourage the behaviour. The euphemism, Eve teasing, is a term which originated from India, Bangladesh and Pakistan meaning sexual harrassment or molestation of women by men. Eve teasing ranges in severity, from sexually suggestive remarks to outright groping. Awareness of the problem is growing throughout the subcontinent. The UAE police offers a series of seminars and public awareness campaigns against Eve teasing. Between 2003 and 2006, 127 Eve teasers were arrested. Those who were nationals were given psychological counselling while non-nationals were deported.

THE BUREAUCRACY

The administrative system in the UAE was borrowed from other Arab countries and is rather complex. Many people are employed in jobs that are superfluous by some standards. All the extra help results in a lot of red tape. This means some documents you must obtain will need to be stamped and signed by many people who will barely even glance at what they are

You should get your business done in the first half of the day, while employees are at their most productive. If at all possible, have someone who has been through it accompany you through the process.

signing half the time. The other half of the time they will examine your papers carefully and make you wait in order to show you how important they are. When this happens you might cope with it by observing how creatively it is done. The process of applying for telephone services, obtaining driving licenses, making large purchases and requesting complex services consume large blocks of time as a result.

Women may get through lines more quickly as they are often sent to the front of the line or taken aside to be served by another woman.

POST OFFICE

Postage is expensive, but the service is reliable. Letters usually take less than one week to arrive at overseas destinations and a matter of days within the country. The post office is one of the few places open straight through the day. Official hours are from 8:00 am to 6:00 pm, Saturday through Thursday, and lines are often long. Men will want to go from 2:00 pm to 5:00 pm when lines are short or non-existent, or else they could have a female friend mail their letters. If there are no postal workers present, wait. They have probably gone to pray and will return in 10–15 minutes. Mail is delivered to post office boxes usually located at one's place of employment. Packages will not be delivered. You will receive a notice of receipt of a package. You have to pick it up at the post office and take it through customs. They will search your package for questionable material as described previously.

POLICE

The police should not be an intrusive presence in your life unless you give them cause to be. They are occasionally encountered driving taxis, which gives them a different observation point. If one picks you up after you've had too much to drink, sober up and behave yourself as being drunk in public is illegal.

When you need emergency assistance, provide the dispatcher with a detailed description of their location and the type of emergency. Many streets are not identified by name, and residences are not numbered. Identifying landmarks or businesses near the location is essential in helping emergency personnel to respond.

Police arriving in response to a report of a crime will not provide the same level of service as in other countries. Most police officers below the rank of lieutenant are expatriates, do not speak English and are hesitant to make independent decisions. Police officers who do speak English are generally assigned to the Criminal Investigation Division. When dialling the police department, ask to speak to an English-speaking officer. Locating an English-speaking officer may take longer on weekends.

> In matters of life and death, policemen cannot be relied upon to risk injury or death to address a possible life-threatening situation. They will look to an Emirati police supervisor to make a decision.

Investigative resources are available locally with sophisticated equipment at hand to assist investigation. The UAE is implementing the use of iris scan technology to create a registry of expatriates from developing countries. Criminals convicted of serious crimes are deported upon the completion of their sentence. This reduces the incidence of recidivism.

PAYMENT

How you pay for items and services depends on where you are. Markets and small businesses usually only take cash. You may write cheques off your local bank account for utilities such as the telephone, at hotels and at some businesses that sell large items such as appliances, furniture, curtains and carpets. Your use of a cheque may get a reaction (a frown or a smile since they are so infrequently used). Credit cards are always welcome at hotels and stores selling gold or carpets.

Smart Cards

The use of credit cards has become more prevalent and the UAE has developed a smart card to function as an all-in-one card that will replace labour, residency and health cards. Smart cards also act as an e-gate, ATM card and an e-passport when crossing into other GCC countries. To

combat fraud, the card with two 64-kilobyte chips, has a three-factor authentication—password, smart card and biometrics, a fingerprint and an iris scan. The iris scan was seen as necessary because there is concern among some Emiratis that the rough hands of labourers do not produce good prints, nor do those of older people because they believe fingerprints may wear down. Scientific evidence however is clear that fingerprints after the age of about 14 never change, though interestingly eye colour can. The smart card system is intended to help enhance homeland security, secure borders, minimise identity theft, improve access and delivery of public service, develop a national population database and help government keep track of expatriates. The government wants cardholders to use the cards to authenticate themselves when they conduct e-government services. The Emiratis can implement the system regardless of public sentiment which has prevented its implementation in other countries where the main concern has been for personal privacy.

SHOPPING

Food can be purchased in grocery stores such as Spinney's or Choithram's or in the *souks*. The grocery stores offer good variety and prices. They may even have more of a variety than you are used to at home because goods are shipped in from all parts of the world. The open-air markets sell local fruits, vegetables, fish and meat, incense and herbs used for medicinal purposes. You can purchase spices at one of the many *souks* which specialise in selling a rich variety including cloves, cardamom, cinnamon, incense, dried fruit and nuts. These goods are sold straight out of open sacks that surround the shops and have a wonderful aroma.

Purchase fish early in the day because it does spoil in the heat. There are many different kinds of fish to choose from; most will probably be unfamiliar to you. Stationary stores sell plastic fish charts to help you identify what you see, and experimenting with all the different kinds can be fun. Once you've purchased your whole fish, you take it to a nearby 'gutter' to have it cleaned.

Red meat is cut directly from the fresh carcass as you order it. Most Westerners prefer to purchase meat in the grocery stores where it is prepackaged. Dry goods such as household wares are purchased in indoor *souks* or small stores located on all the major and minor streets everywhere.

Traditional shopping is a great tourist attraction as goods are clustered in *souks*. There is a gold *souk* in Dubai which boasts one of the largest retail gold markets in the world. Everything sold here is gold from ingots to intricately worked

A store displaying a large collection of gold jewellery.

jewellery and all for bargain prices. The store windows glitter with all the gold. You can find old rugs, weapons and jewellery, scarves, incense burners and imported treasures from India in the designated shops. Other individually owned and operated shops sell books, shoes, clothes and so on.

Modern shopping centres abound in Dubai and Abu Dhabi and have become very popular destinations not just for shopping but also for socialising. This is creating a decrease in shopping activity for the small independent shops, and more traditional shopping areas are liable to disappear in time.

Both Dubai and Abu Dhabi boast duty free shops at their international airports that are making record-breaking profits. 'Duty free' does not equate with low prices; it means, rather, that high-quality goods can be sold for prices that do not include duty costs or taxes. This is a bit of an oxymoron in a country where most goods can be purchased tax and duty free anyway. Open ports with low import duties and no taxation enable the UAE to offer bargain hunting with unbeatable value. The quantity and quality of goods is unbelievable, and often products are even less expensive than in their country of origin.

Shopping Festival

Every year between December and February, Dubai is host to the Shopping Festival. Since 1996 this shopping and entertainment mega-event has been marketed worldwide. In 1996 1.6 million visitors spent over half a billion US dollars in six weeks. A decade later, 3.5 million people spent close to US$ 3 billion within the same timeframe. It is ironic the phonetic pronunciation of Dubai is the imperative 'do buy'!

Bargaining

Customers are expected to bargain, especially in the *souks*. Shopkeepers and vendors may drop prices dramatically. If they won't, move on—you will find the same item elsewhere. There is no hard and fast rule for how much of a percentage is to come down when bargaining, but retail prices can be dropped significantly. Bargaining is a time-honoured tradition in this part of the world. Decide what you are willing to pay for an item and walk away from the deal if you cannot get your price. Never be rude. Bargaining is considered fun and is expected; politeness and amiability are part of the process. In the *souks* start bargaining at about half the stated price. When you have agreed to a price this is considered a verbal contract and you are expected to buy. The sales people are expert at bargaining and will close the deal when they sense weakness on your part.

Away from the *souks* and in stores with set prices, bargaining is less common. One way to bargain is to hold an item, point to the price, and ask, "Is this before discount?" The answer may be negative, indicating the price is final, but then again you may get 10 or 15 per cent off the price. It is worth a try.

Souvenirs

In a nomadic culture such as that of the Bedouin, items are portable, and thus many traditional items are easy to pack, making great presents. Prices and quality of traditional items vary greatly depending on where you buy them, from the roadside vendor or from the hotel boutique. The *souk* is usually the best place to get a variety of both price and quality.

The traditional items you might consider bringing home are the coffee pot and cups, wooden carvings, prayer beads, the *khanjar*—a short curved knife in a sheath, jewellery, carpets and gold.

Tipping

Tipping is not expected, but is common practice with 10 per cent being a standard amount. Gratuities to staff at hotels are at your discretion. Most restaurants add service charges to the bill (Abu Dhabi 16 per cent; Sharjah 15 per cent; Dubai 10 per cent). If this charge is not included, add 10 per cent of the total to the bill. Taxi drivers do not expect to be tipped but greatly appreciate it. Supermarket baggers, bag carriers and windscreen washers at petrol stations are generally given 2 dhs.

Clothes

There are countless tailors whose labour is incredibly inexpensive. Men and women can have Western suits made to fit for US$ 40 or less (not including the cost of material). Choose your material carefully, it should be heavy or light enough for what you are having made. Your tailor will make the garment you request whether you've chosen the right material or not, and you will have to pay for it. While the choice of material is up to you, a good fit is up to the tailor. You should not pay for a garment until you are happy with the way it fits. Once you have paid, the tailor will not touch the item again. This applies for other services as well as tailoring, so be sure you are satisfied before you pay.

Ready-made garments are available, though they are considerably more expensive than tailor-made clothes. Anything from top designer and straight off the runway to ready-made bargain basement piles of clothes are available from all over the world. Very popular and available everywhere are the traditional saris. These are made of silk or cotton, fibres which are excellent in the desert heat. They can be dressy or casual. While dressing in the sari is perhaps the most comfortable of all the choices, this outfit is seldom worn by Western women.

OUTDOORS
Dress Code

Although the dress code in the UAE is generally casual, guests in the larger hotels do tend to dress more formally in the evening. If you are dressing for a night on the town, bare shoulders and form fitting gowns are common for women, and men will wear nice suits or even tuxedos. Your trendiest clothing will be perfect for wearing to the discos and you will want to have plenty of clothing for exercising.

Dressing is more conservative where there are likely to be Emiratis or other Middle Eastern and Eastern men, such as at the movie theatres, shopping centres, *souks* and in the villages and towns of the smaller emirates. If you are in doubt as to what to wear, cover your arms, legs and cleavage, and wear loose fitting clothing. Lightweight summer clothing is ideal with a wrap, sweater or jacket for cooler winter nights and air-conditioned premises.

Beaches

With few exceptions, the UAE's population is concentrated on the coast. Outside of the cities people can walk or drive on the beaches wherever they please. Dressing should be conservative, particularly if you are alone or with only one or two other people. In a group, while you may be watched, you will be left alone. Married women are fortunate to have a man with them, and life is easier for them in this respect. Single women would do well to travel with a friend.

Within the city limits there are public beaches. While it is legal for you to go to these beaches, it can be uncomfortable. They tend to be frequented by single subcontinent men, though these men are occasionally accompanied by their families. The women wisely stay covered. The men strip down to their underwear (briefs) to swim. Westerners are so outnumbered at these public beaches it is uncomfortable to go because they are stared at by everyone. Expatriate women may have a particularly bad time because even in male company they receive undue attention.

Women alone anywhere in the UAE are likely to attract unwanted attention. Put on a bikini and such attention will increase dramatically.

Lifeguards have two focuses—people drowning and women being ogled at. There are beach security teams from the police departments and they are quite responsive, particularly during weekends and holidays when their patrols are increased.

Hotels offer an expensive option. They provide towels, beach umbrellas, showers and even hot tubs. Their beaches are clean and enclosed by wire mesh and harassment is virtually unheard of within their designated and gated area. Since you are visiting a Muslim country, bikinis, swimsuits, shorts and revealing tops should be confined to beach resorts. Note that in Sharjah women are prohibited from wearing swimsuits on public beaches.

Public Beach Picks

Some public beaches charge by car or by pedestrian. Good beach choices in Dubai are Jumeirah Beach Park and Al Mamzar Park, both featuring beautifully landscaped gardens alongside an expanse of protected beach. Each offers women and children-only days and times. These beaches are kept clean and have a comfortable mix of people using them. Many families as well as a balanced mix of men and women go there, so harassment is less of a problem.

Public Restrooms

In the past, the women used to go out into the desert in one group and the men in another twice a day—once at dawn and once at dusk, when the light was fading and they could not be seen. Now public restrooms are as available everywhere as they are in any developed country. Most shopping centres, public gardens, museums and so on have clean, well-maintained public toilets with a choice of toilet paper or water for cleaning. Public toilets in *souks* and bus stations may be just for men.

The toilets are of two types. First there is the Eastern porcelain bowl inlaid in the ground. There are spaces for your feet on either side of the bowl. These are found outside of the cities at restaurants and petrol stations, and they may

not be clean. In these restrooms, toilet paper is almost never available (though water is) because it is assumed people use water and their left hand to clean themselves. For this reason, eating is done with the right hand and things are given and received with the right hand only. Westerners usually carry a supply of tissue paper when travelling. The other type is the pedestal-style toilet 'seat.' As with many borrowed Western conveniences, the 'seat' was originally adopted not for its usefulness, but simply because it is Western. Both styles of toilet may be available at public places within the cities. Where only the Western style is available, footprints on the toilet seats will show how things borrowed from the West are adapted.

Photography

Film is readily available, so too are processing facilities and colour prints are produced in record time. Do not take photographs of airports, docks, industrial or military sites, government buildings or telecommunications equipment. Be sensitive when taking pictures of people. Always ask permission. Men should not take photographs of women, especially not the Emirati women. While photographs of people can be difficult to obtain, photographs of the scenery and animals are not. Many amateur photographers have found endless fascinating subjects to photograph in the UAE, and have honed their photographic skills there.

HEALTH

The UAE government has had modern hospitals built, equipped them with the latest medical instruments and staffed them entirely with Western doctors. These new hospitals provide healthcare for the Emiratis entirely free of charge. Staff in hospitals are accustomed to the Emirati women not wanting to undress for male physicians, or male patients for female physicians. Western female doctors are in great demand. When an Emirati has to be admitted to the hospital for care, he or she is accompanied by the entire family who camp out in the patient's room and in the halls.

Foreigners can obtain lists of recommended doctors and dentists from their consulate. Colleagues will be sure to have their own recommendations. The major hospitals have emergency rooms. Pharmacies abound in every city and the Gulf News runs the list of pharmacies open for 24 hours on a particular day. This list changes regularly. Many employers provide health insurance.

Some optional vaccinations you may want to get are typhoid, tetanus and poliomyelitis. Polio has been eliminated from the UAE. Cholera is not a problem in the country and the cholera vaccine is purported not to be terribly effective anyway. You do not have to worry about plague, but there are many feral cats, some of which carry rabies. They search for their food in the garbage bins. Try to avoid them. Some accounts advise you to take precautions against malaria. In three years though, I only knew one person to come down with malaria and he got it on a vacation in Madagascar. The UAE is too hot and dry most of the year to be a breeding ground for mosquitos. Check with your embassy or airline for a government advisory regarding the current situation.

People who live in developing countries for a long time develop immunities and can relax some of their eating and drinking practices. Short-time travellers do not have time to do so.

Hepatitis A is a possibility, but the vaccine lasts such a short time (two to six months depending on the strength of the dose) it is often not worth bothering about. Hepatitis A, diarrhoea and food poisoning may result from poor food hygiene or poor sanitation. Avoid eating food from fly-infested restaurants. Drink bottled water—it is worth the cost to be safe.

Brucellosis is an illness carried by cattle and transmitted to humans through milk. Proper milk pasteurization will kill the germ, but out in the desert milk is brought straight from the animal to the dinner table. When you are offered tea or coffee in the desert, accept the coffee. Tea is usually served with milk while the traditional Arabic coffee is not. When the germ is transmitted, it results in undulant or Maltese fever, characterised by a general malaise and hot and cold shivers similar to malaria. It is usually not fatal, but neither is it curable; like malaria, it will recur throughout one's life.

Food hygiene and water are of extremely high quality, especially in all of the populated areas. Avoid raw salads and *shawarmas* (meat cooked on a spit and served in a pita bread sandwich) if you are at all concerned.

Water is usually produced by desalination and is normally safe to drink, but from time to time it may not be so. You can never know what might accidentally get in it. Water is sometimes stored in tanks on roofs. If the tanks are not clean, worms, bacteria and other visible intruders will come out of your water faucet. There was one year when many people in Abu Dhabi began complaining of an inordinate amount of hair loss. The government stopped using a new water purification chemical they'd been experimenting with and the hair loss complaints stopped. It is advisable to drink plenty of water in the heat, so carry a bottle with you at all times.

Traditional Remedies

Many Emiratis use herbs, seeds, roots, spices, plants and prayer to heal ailments. For example, a concoction made of thyme, fenugreek, frankincense and *kheel* is used to clear constipation. Frankincense by itself is eaten to cure a stomachache, or burned so the smoke can cure a headache. When all attempts to heal an ailing person fail, a fire-healer may be called in to brand an afflicted person. The fire healer applies the tip of a hot rod to an ulcerated or infected area. These practices are still common among villagers and old people and some remedies may always be trusted over other methods throughout the society.

EDUCATION

Expatriates with school-age children have numerous choices among the many private schools. Each school caters to a specific clientele and offers a curriculum similar to one found in the foreigner's home country. Some schools require students pass a screening process before they are admitted. Restrictions such as country of origin can also affect admission. Schools offer many after-school activities, from Scouts to sports to tournaments and competitions held in neighbouring countries. However, their exclusivity can limit them in providing cross-cultural opportunities. Often students of other nationalities attending a British or American school are highly Westernised.

Settling down in Dubai and Abu Dhabi looks easy on the surface because everything is available. It is easy to be lulled into thinking you are not in transition. Schools and organisations offer orientation programmes to assist newcomers. Parents who involve themselves more in their children's lives, interests and projects may be more successful at keeping their children out of trouble just as they would be in their home country. Select a school that best meets the needs of your children.

As in many societies, finding the best education is important, but it can be challenging and expensive. Tuition fees can be as much as US$ 10,000 per year. Many companies foot this fee for their employees. In fact, some companies buy blocks of space in a school for the children of anticipated newly-arriving employees. Find out in advance; it certainly isn't a fee you want to be paying out of your own pocket. Services for children with physical or mental disabilities are almost non-existent, particularly in higher grades. There are many quality challenges in education in the UAE.

The UAE government provides elementary and secondary education, but private education tends to be superior to that offered in the public sector and so the number of students in private education outnumbers those in public education. Children of expatriates also may attend government schools for a fee.

Government School Woes

Government schools receive poor marks in general. Of the nearly 750 public schools in the country, 60 per cent of them were deemed unacceptable in a report commissioned by the Ministry of Education (MOE) in 2007. US consulting firm MGT estimated US$ 350 million was needed to maintain existing buildings and nearly US$ 11 billion was needed to build new ones. One of the biggest complaints is the lack of gymnasium facilities. Schools built before the year 2000 do not have gyms, as those were not included in construction plans. It is too hot to exercise outside. Obesity and diabetes are common health problems among the youth as a result.

Other problems include inadequate laboratories, scarce equipment, insufficient computers and library resource materials, lack of ventilation, faulty air-conditioning, and too few English teachers and administrative staff. Many of the schools are over 25 years old and even the walls need to be replaced. The problem is so widespread that when possible, parents enrol their children in private schools.

Higher Education

More has been invested recently in higher education and most UAE nationals pursue a college degree. The Higher Colleges of Technology (HCT) have 14 schools in the UAE, and are respected for their innovative learning so much so that companies such as Microsoft, Shell and Cisco Systems

Education System Overview

- Education free to UAE nationals from primary through higher education.
- Four-tiers of compulsory education up to grade nine—kindergarten, primary school (ages 6–11), preparatory stage (ages 12–14) and secondary school (ages 15–17).
- Aim for 90 per cent of teachers to be Emiratis by 2020, so as to maintain Islamic principles and traditions.
- 90 per cent of women and 80 per cent of men continue from high school into higher education, one of the highest rates of college attainment in the world.
- The Ministry of Higher Education monitors higher education and approves admissions to its undergraduate institutions.
- Largest institutions are the United Arab Emirates University, Zayed University, the Higher Colleges of Technology (14 schools in the UAE), Gulf Medical College and University of Sharjah.
- Private universities and colleges include the American Universities of Sharjah and Dubai and the Ajman University of Science and Technology.
- In medicine, world-class institutions have centres set up in the UAE including Johns Hopkins and Cleveland Clinic.
- Knowledge Village in Dubai Free Zone holds campuses for many foreign universities.
- Knowledge Village has over 6,000 students, 25 per cent of which are from Middle Eastern countries, attending training and education established by 200 companies. Students obtain undergraduate, post-graduate, MBA and PhD degrees in computing, technology, medicine, telecommunications, fashion and business.
- Over US$ 3 billion will have been invested in Knowledge Village by 2012 to house 20 or more universities and serve 30,000 to 40,000 students.

have partnered with HCT to provide training and development programmes. The University of Washington, the Sorbonne, Harvard, and American University are some of the forerunners in establishing close relationships and campuses in the UAE, offering education and degrees comparable to those students can obtain in the US. The government funds the Emiratis' attendance at these schools, and students of other nationalities may receive generous scholarships that help with their tuition expenses.

The UAE is determined to improve education and research across all sectors. In technology the Higher Colleges of Technology have a commercial arm called the Centre of Excellence for Applied Research and Training (CERT). Through strategic alliances with Intel, Microsoft, IBM and other industry leaders CERT has created a fully-integrated community of research, innovation and entrepreneurship, and shares of this education and technology IPO can be purchased by investors.

All UAE citizens have a wide selection of educational institutions within the country. This is critical for women who are less likely than men to be granted permission by their families to study abroad. Emirati women outnumber and outperform men in education at all levels partly because they are anxious to play a part in their country's development and are determined not to be left behind.

HOUSING

Your sponsor should provide housing for you. Consider this issue up front when you are negotiating your contract. Housing is limited and the cost of rental is high. In addition, housing is often paid in six-month or one-year lump sums, though there are some apartment complexes that are rented out on a month-to-month basis. Prices have skyrocketed and in response the government formed a regulating body called the Real Estate Regulatory Authority (RERA) in Dubai to oversee the entire sector for the emirate. All real estate companies and agents are required to be registered with this authority and all documents in relation to a sale or rental must be provided. The government has strictly capped

While the UAE is one of the safest places in the world to visit, expatriates are known to have long vacations and their houses may be watched and robbed while they are gone. As this happens all too frequently, insurance agents may allow coverage where tenants may only be gone for a one-month period in a year.

rental rates to no more than a 7 per cent annual increase. If using an agent to find a rental, a 5 per cent commission fee is expected. One-year contracts are typical but contracts can be for up to three years. Once the contract is signed, the landlord cannot raise the rent or add extra charges for anything not agreed to in the original contract.

Sharjah, only a 20-minute drive from Dubai, is an affordable option for expatriates who work in Dubai. Apartments in Sharjah are considerably less expensive and more readily available, though the commute to Dubai is about the worst in the UAE and must be taken into consideration. Also consider that Sharjah is a dry emirate (meaning the commercial sale of alcohol is completely prohibited), so the night life is tame compared to Dubai.

Expatriates mainly live in villas or apartments. Buildings are constructed of concrete. Workmanship tends to be poor and electrical fires sometimes occur within the walls, causing smoke damage. Doors and windows are numerous and not

well set, and keeping sand out of the house is a daily battle. Floor plans are improving with new construction, but many places are laid out with a hall as the central area with rooms set off from it here and there. This is not conducive to entertaining, something many expatriates do a great deal of here.

The UAE began to allow freehold ownership in 2002 in designated areas. With the availability of long-term visas and mortgages, these have proven extremely popular and successful with foreigners throughout the Gulf. Wealthy people from all over the world come to buy high-end residential homes, often as second homes.

There are challenges to buying real estate in the UAE, beginning with real estate agents. Agents have no licensing requirements. Visit the agent's office and make sure the agent is experienced, professional and registered locally. Before buying anything, make sure you have seen genuine ownership documents and passport copies so you know you are paying the real owner and not a con artist. Engage the services of a lawyer—there are many who speak both English and Arabic and come highly recommended.

Electricity

Only 220-volt electricity is available. You can purchase electrical converters if you have small 110-volt appliances. Appliances used this way have a short life span though and you may eventually end up purchasing new appliances using 220 volts. Appliances purchased in the UAE will generally have two-pin plugs attached. Bathrooms may not have outlets in them but more frequently are included in newer construction. Sockets suitable for three-pin 13 amp plugs are usual. Adaptors can be purchased in local supermarkets.

Furniture

In the 1980s Emirati taste, being new and less sophisticated, tended to favour glitz and one would be hard-pressed to find a bedroom set that did not have flashing neon lights and a stereo system in the headboard. Nowadays there is almost unlimited choice and the Emirati taste is highly sophisticated. You can find any type of furniture, from second-hand to

IKEA to designer made. You can furnish your house in old Portuguese carved wood furnishings or wicker. You can search the 'nickel ads' or save up for the finest money can buy.

A few entrepreneurs have caught on to the idea that Westerners like antiques. They are manufacturing them at a great rate and charging increasingly higher prices for them. Look around, however, and you might actually be able to find some treasures that others have considered to be junk and thrown out. These treasures are complemented well with a few Persian carpets purchased at the Sharjah *souk*.

Pets

To an Emirati, a camel is an ideal pet while Westerners tend to favour cats and dogs. Your pet is welcome in the UAE but your landlord may not allow them. Also, in summer the temperature is often so high, cats and dogs are uncomfortable outdoors.

In the early 1990s I walked in and out of the country several times a year with my cat in a carry-on conveyance. Now pets must be shipped as cargo and this can be expensive. Contact an airline to arrange for shipment. You will need an import permit, your pet will need a microchip with the microchip number, (a ten or 15-digit ISO) which must appear on all documents, a Good Health Certificate from your veterinarian on letterhead with the name, age, breed, colour and gender of the pet. This certificate must state that your pet is free of rabies and healthy enough to travel. The certificate must include your pet's microchip number, be signed and stamped by your veterinarian and by the veterinarian of the national government of the exporting country. The certificate travels with your pet (keep a copy for yourself) and is issued no more than ten days before travel.

Finally, you will need a vaccination certificate showing a valid rabies vaccination and your pet's microchip number. This too must be signed and stamped by your veterinarian. Submit copies of all these documents via fax to the person handling your employment and they will forward records to the Ministry of Environment and Water (MEW). MEW inspects the certificate and issues an import permit valid for 60 days. Animals must be examined within 48 hours prior to their arrival in the UAE and be certified as being free of any evidence of infectious or contagious diseases and external parasites. Have this certificate sent with the pet or bring it with you. Only the person in whose name the pets are shipped may pick up the pet. Go to the cargo section of the airport to collect your pet and bring the original import permit, the original vaccination certificate, and a photocopy of your passport. There is no quarantine period in the UAE so you will be able to take your pet directly home. Do not forget to investigate the laws governing the return of your pet to your home country. The return may be complex enough to deter you from importing your pet in the first place.

MEDIA

Dubai has established Dubai Media City, a tax-free zone intended to boost the UAE's media presence in news agencies, publishing, online media, advertising, production and broadcasting. Major broadcasters based at Dubai Media City include APTN, Associated Press, BBC World, Bloomberg, CNBC Arabiya, CNN, Reuters, and Voice of America, to name a few.

For the most part broadcasters are free to report on local and regional events, but there is always the potential they will be shut down, as happened during the Pakistani political turmoil of late 2007 at the request of Pakistan's General Pervez Musharraf. When broadcast resumed, coverage by at least two stations was noticeably different, highlighting that freedom of the press is a privilege and not a right in the UAE.

Internet

The UAE government is the sole Internet service provider via Etisalat and Du, and is able to censor the Internet. It does so to protect political, moral and religious values and this is popular among the nationals who view it as an effective measure to protect family members from objectionable content. The UAE uses the SmartFilter filtering software to block pornography, gambling, religious conversion, the Israeli top-level domain, Bahai faith, Middle East-oriented gay and lesbian sites, English-language dating sites and illegal drugs sites. Allowed are Arabic-language dating sites, political sites, and news and media sources. Broadband service is expensive, as much as five times the cost in Europe. Even with the introduction of Du as competition to Etisalat, prices have not come down.

Print Media

The two major English newspapers, the *Kaleej Times* and the *Gulf News*, are available in English or Arabic, and you can have them delivered to your house.

The *Gulf News* has a colour supplement that gives pictures and information on expatriate activities. It focuses on a different city or emirate each day of the week.

Excellent coverage of events in the emirates is found in *What's On*, a substantial magazine serving both the UAE and Oman.

Also available are foreign-based newspapers, *The Times* of London and *The Sunday Times*.

Some Available Local Newspapers And Magazines

- *Gulf News*: Highest-circulating newspaper in the UAE.
- *Khaleej Times*: Second in circulation behind *Gulf News*.
- *Emirates Today*: A government-owned newspaper.
- *Xpress*: A tabloid published weekly by *Gulf News*.
- *What's On*: A popular and lowly-priced monthly UAE-based magazine covering entertainment and leisure.
- *7Days*: Highest-circulating tabloid providing news as well as local and regional perspectives.

Freedom Of The Press

The government censors the written news. It is currently forbidden to write against the government or anyone in authority. Reports of crime must be approved by the police, and civil protests are written about with great care. Mainstream publishing is owned and controlled by the government, which makes it extremely difficult to be constructively critical of the people who hire the writers and editors. The UAE government recognises the urgency in updating and transforming the publication law of the UAE in favour of greater freedom of press and transparency.

Removing corruption and making significant progress up the international transparency ladder are stated UAE goals, and so a law has been proposed. This law states that violations such as libel would not be considered a criminal act.

In 2007, the editors of local newspapers signed a code of ethics with 26 articles defining the rules and ethics of the profession. The code of ethics calls for respecting the truth and the right of the public to have access to true and accurate information; respecting privacy of individuals, and demanding that journalists commit themselves to the principle of innocent until proven guilty; respecting law and order; upholding freedom, equality, and ethics; and prohibiting the targeting of religious beliefs of individuals. The proposed law and the code of ethics represent great strides of progress within the culture.

Television

Many people, even the Emiratis, have satellite dishes on the roofs of their buildings. Channels they can beam in 24 hours a day are Al Jazeera, Arabsat, Star TV, VTV, CNN and the BBC with the exception of Arabsat, which goes off the air at midnight or 1:00 am. Of course, there is no way to censor these channels, so censorship is up to the discretion of the viewer. With the proliferation of the Internet, the extensive censorship evident in the past is becoming next to impossible.

Al Jazeera, a satellite network news channel, has emerged as a source of news on the Middle East portraying the image of the Arab world from the Arab point of view. Al Jazeera provides an English channel and its exhaustive coverage of the region is noted and used by Western news sources. The Arab world has regained some of its self-confidence in being able to portray itself through Al Jazeera. People everywhere are concerned the media does not allow for intelligent, critical thinking and that freedom of expression and entertainment have resulted in a culture of mediocrity and agitation over instantaneous news. To avoid this, Al Jazeera set up a research centre to provide in-depth analysis of the media itself. Still, it is in danger of becoming a tool for propaganda as is every other similar medium in every other country. What has emerged of grave concern for Western media establishments is Al Jazeera's ability to portray crimes by the West which the West had until now been able to prevent from being made public or to slant favourably.

SINGLES AND MARRIEDS

The UAE, Dubai in particular, is a Gulf playground. 'Swinging single' Westerners from their late teens through their 30s abound. They seem to be having a wonderful time bouncing from one party to the next, but are they? Living in a Club Med-like atmosphere eventually grows old and boredom takes hold.

Married people and people with families have responsibilities to each other. These responsibilities give their lives structure and they are able to support each other. Couples can face their difficulties together with someone they love and trust while single people don't readily have this luxury. An added bonus for married women is that they have an ever-present male escort to shelter them from some of the hardships single women encounter. However, the marriage bears the stress of living overseas. Couples either grow closer together or further apart.

> Married people too frequently make the mistake of thinking the singles' lives are so much more interesting and exciting than their dull stay-at-home existence.

Wives who do not work (and more frequently of late, husbands) are at home and alone too much. The maid does the housework and the boredom becomes unbearable. Couples need to be aware of the extra stress before they arrive in order to decide together how best to cope with it. Making friends and spending time with other couples while avoiding the singles scene is advisable.

THE SHORT-TIMER'S ATTITUDE

People who have decided to leave the UAE sometimes develop a short-timer's attitude, even if their leave date is six months or more away. They stop making friends and begin to distance themselves from the people and activities around them. A few people have this attitude right from the beginning of their stay and keep it no matter how many

years they remain in the UAE. Their negativity about their environment can be particularly intense in their effort to cope with and maintain their transient state.

ADVICE FOR COPING

Adjusting will be facilitated by reading about the Emiratis, and building interest in them and their country. Also, understanding the cultural meanings behind your daily frustrations will cause them to be less infuriating. The neighbouring Oman offers you endless hours of exploration of yet another culture if the one you are in never quite opens up to you. It is a beautiful place to travel in as well.

See yourself as being fortunate to live in a place where you can learn about so many different people. View your friendships as permanent. Learn a little Arabic. You are not expected to know much or do well with it, but Arabs will be flattered that you tried. It is not difficult to learn a dozen or so very useful phrases either.

Focus on the positive aspects of the environment and spend time with other positively focused people. Finally, lower your expectations of yourself and others. Allow more time to accomplish errands or to complete projects, especially in the beginning when you are adjusting. Whether you realise it or not, you are under additional stress and you constantly need to take care of yourself.

CHAPTER 6

FOOD IN THE UAE

'Eat of garlic until you are full
Eat of onions what you can find
Eat of radish tails as a habit.'
—UAE proverb

RESTAURANTS

The three major cities in the UAE have a selection of restaurants ranging from a corner juice shop serving fruit shakes to those serving fine Italian cuisine. Of course, choice of food and location of the restaurant are reflected in price. One of the best meals I've eaten was a breakfast of two large meat and egg sandwiches and three cups of coffee at a roadside hut for about US$ 0.50. Fast food restaurants will cost from US$ 7 to $ 15 per person and an expensive meal with spirits could run from US$ 40 per person to hundreds of dollars. This is not exorbitant given the high salaries earned by foreigners, but then it is not something to be done everyday.

Here Come The Fast Food Chains

Up until early 1995, you could not find a McDonald's restaurant because it is a Jewish corporation (Israel and Judaism are censored as completely as possible from the country because of the ongoing strife with Israel). Money did eventually open the doors to the chain and now everyone can order a burger and fries in any of the big cities. Elsewhere in the country however, one is unlikely to find much other than roadside huts serving Indian cuisine, if any at all.

Family Section

Restaurants usually have family sections. These are upstairs or tucked out of sight. Single men, primarily labourers, are

Women do not have to sit in secluded areas, but in some restaurants, the male staff will be uncomfortable with a woman's decision to dine in the main area and will communicate that to her through looks and extremely fast service.

not allowed in these parts of the restaurant and the intent of the separation is to provide women with as much privacy and segregation as possible while in public. The secluded sections may make women feel more comfortable in public as they can't be stared at when they are tucked away.

MEAL TIMES

Breakfast is eaten between 6:30 am and 7:30 am, before work or school. Work stops between 1:00 p.m. and 4:00 pm or 4:30 pm. During this time the Emiratis, labourers, bankers and shopkeepers eat their lunch and sleep. This custom is the most sensible for the labourers who are mercifully allowed to rest while the sun is at its hottest.

Many foreigners working in the oil industry or education sector follow a Western schedule and only take an hour for lunch with work finishing for the day at 5:00 pm. Those with a longer lunch break resume work in the afternoon and work until 8:30 pm or 9:00 pm, after which they have a small dinner. This is a schedule similar to that found in many Mediterranean countries and a healthy one, given the local

Friends of mixed gender enjoy a meal together in a Dubai restaurant.

climate. In many ways the difference in schedules is useful for the Westerners since they can still run errands or shop after work. Furthermore, the UAE is four to 12 hours ahead of the Western countries they do business with, and a change in schedule would not facilitate communications with them. Emiratis eat dinner later than Westerners are accustomed to doing, as late as 11:00 pm or midnight. However, restaurants typically follow a Western schedule of serving dinner from 6:00 pm to 10:00 pm.

The Fualah

In addition to the three meals of breakfast, lunch and dinner, Emiratis also eat two other small meals called *fualah*. One of these meals is eaten between breakfast and lunch, and the other is eaten between lunch and dinner. The *fualah* is a ritualistic meal performed for visitors because it enables the hostess to perform her duty of seeing the visit extend into a meal.

The *fualah* is also performed for festive events such as the birth of a child, religious feasts, the circumcision of a boy and weddings. The food served consists of a variety of fruits, sweets, nuts and coffee. Perfumes and incense are also passed around as part of the ritual. Incense is placed in burners, lit and fanned until it is burning well enough to produce wafts of smoke. The burners are then placed under raised legs, dresses are drawn tightly around the legs, then the *abaya* (black cloak) is securely draped over this so the women can absorb as much smoke as possible. If a woman is wearing a skirt and blouse, she will stand over the burner and pull her waistband away from her waist so the aroma can reach her blouse and hair. The women enjoy using perfumes, incense and dyes that are artistic or seductive. They are always applied to clean the skin after a shower or ablutions for prayer.

RAMADAN SCHEDULE

During the holy month of Ramadan, dining and sleeping schedules change drastically and Westerners are affected by the changes. Arabs eat before sunrise and after sundown but fast in between, taking neither food nor drink. Arabs' religious

awareness is greatly heightened during this month and the Emiratis are far less tolerant of blatant deviation from their customs. It is illegal to be seen drinking or eating in public during daylight hours. Bars are closed or tucked away from offending sight. Restaurants outside of the hotels are closed until sunset and the blast of a cannon signals the breaking of the fast. This is called *iftar*. Most restaurants serve an elaborate buffet. Guests are poised over the buffet table and when the cannon sounds, signalling the fast may be broken, they dive in, piling as much food as they can onto their plates. This is not a time for reticence if one wishes to get something to eat; do not allow yourself to be pushed out of line in the frenzy.

GULF CUISINE

Emiratis eat many foods that are similar to non-Gulf Arab selections such as lamb, chicken and mutton cooked whole or prepared as *kebabs* (meat and vegetable skewers cooked over an open flame) and served on rice with a tomato and vegetable sauce. However, their other dishes are unique in that most of them are sweetened with the sugar from dates (their most abundant agricultural crop). *Bilaleet* is a dish of cold vermicelli noodles, sweetened and served with a hot, flat omelette on top. Pieces of the omelette are used to pick up the sticky vermicelli to eat. *Harees* is a paste of lamb and cracked wheat. Rice and meat dishes are flavoured with a mixture of cardamom, coriander, cumin, ginger, turmeric and saffron called *baharat*. Their breads, as with many dishes, are borrowed from cultures the Emiratis have had trade contact with. The flat bread called *mafrooda* is from Persia and *naan* is originally from India.

USING YOUR HANDS

There is a proper etiquette to eating with the hands. Only the right hand is used because food is a gift from God and should be accorded respect. Dip your thumb and first and second fingers into the dish. Make a ball out of the food (this takes practise) and rest this on the two fingers. Push the ball of food off the fingers into the mouth with the thumb. Emirati women are able to do this without removing their *burkas* (veils) or using their left hand. They lift and pop food in with one swift, practised movement.

Quantity, Not Quality

While quality may not matter in Emirati cuisine, quantity does. Two to three times as much food as can be eaten may be prepared as a sign of hospitality. The excess food is not wasted, but is shared with poor people or is eaten by the family and servants in the days to come. If you enquire of an Emirati about a dish or express an appreciation for one, you may be presented with a large quantity of it in a day or two. When you have finished the dish, prepare something from your country and return the full container to the Emirati. One expatriate I knew received a large platter of rice with a whole roasted camel hock in the centre. This is not an uncommon show of hospitality.

In an Emirati home, the family and guests sit on pillows. Guests visit for about two hours before a meal is served and linger about an hour after. It is a good idea to bring your host or hostess something small such as flowers or candy. Guests are served eldest to youngest, with the younger people doing the serving. When guests are present, men and women eat separately. Children are only present if they know the guests well.

The men eat before the women do, but the women do not eat their leftovers. Instead, separate meals are prepared for both groups. A woman may eat with her father, brothers, sons, uncles and nephews when there are no guests. These men are members of her incest group, i.e., those men she cannot marry. If you are a woman and have been invited to dine with the men, be aware that you are considered the entertainment, not the guest.

Food is served in the sleeping or living areas and the *majlis* is used as a dining area only for guests. Food is served in platters on mats on the floor so one is considerably higher than one's food. Everyone eats using their right hand from the same large platters, but these are so big and the amount of food in them so great, neighbours are unlikely to bump into each other.

Some hosts and hostesses may provide guests with a plate and serving utensils with each dish. Go ahead and use them; Emiratis want more than anything for you to feel comfortable. The host or hostess usually serves the guest, who should be prepared with two hands to accept the overflowing plate. It would be rude to refuse. The more food placed on the plate, the greater the honour being shown the guest. This can border on the ridiculous and you should not feel you have to eat more than makes you comfortable. The food is eaten quickly and in silence.

EATING CUSTOMS

Food is seen as one of God's greatest gifts and customs have arisen to reflect this belief. While eating, there is very little talking. However, there are ceremonial sayings at different stages of a meal. Everyone says '*bismillah*' (in the name of God) just prior to eating. During the meal the host or hostess encourages everyone to eat more and says such things as '*billah alaich tihbshi*' (by God you should eat) and '*ma habashtu*' (you did not eat). You may need to indicate you are finished eating several times. When you are really finished say, '*akramch Allah*' (may God honour you) or '*Allah yin'am 'alaich*' (may God bestow his grace on you). The host or hostess will end the meal with '*bil 'afiah*' (to your health) to which you reply '*Allah yilafich/yhannich*' (may God make you healthy and happy, to a man/woman).

Coffee

Coffee is served at the end of the meal. Coffee is the single most significant expression of hospitality in the Emirati culture. You should never refuse a cup as it implies an insult. The coffee will have been freshly-ground, mixed with cardamom and is unsweetened. Nowadays it is commonly poured from a thermos bottle but traditionally it was poured from a *dalla*, a brass pot with a long beak-like nozzle. *Dallas* can be found in the *souks* (markets). The Emiratis view them as junk, but tourists think they are wonderful souvenirs. Shopkeepers price them according to how much they think tourists will pay for them.

The coffee is poured into handle-less demi tasse cups. Only about one-third to half of the small cup is filled. Servers pride themselves on being able to hold enough cups for four to five people in the left hand while pouring and serving all of them without setting the coffee pot down. When you have had enough coffee—at least three helpings—shake the cup from side to side several times, otherwise the server will keep filling your glass.

Two Emirati men drinking coffee in a *majlis,* an important social custom of Arab culture which places great importance on hospitality.

You will almost always be offered coffee or tea when you walk into a business, and always when in someone's home. There is no need to play coy with this group of people—accept it on the first offer. While relaxing over coffee after a meal you should say '*Alhamdulillah*' (praise be to God) to show your contentment. A water bowl and towel may be passed around for everyone to wash their hands.

Playing Host

When inviting Emiratis to your home, inform them whether men and women will be separated, otherwise the man may show up without his wife. Even if men and women are separated, it is unlikely your Emirati guest will bring his wife. Serve a large variety of items to choose from, but do not serve alcohol. If you serve pork, be sure to label the dish so the Muslims among your guests know not to have any.

Encourage them to have seconds and thirds. Do so more than once so that you make them feel welcome, and when they leave for the evening, escort them all the way out of your apartment building or gate to their car. The front door is just not far enough.

NON-GULF ARAB CUISINE

There are numerous Lebanese restaurants in Abu Dhabi and Dubai and a few in Al-Ain. The food and service in these tend to be excellent and reasonably priced. Some dishes on the menu are *shish taouk* and *shish kebab*—skewered meat cooked over a grill; *hoummos*—a puree of chick peas; *tahina* —a sesame paste with lemon juice; *tabbouleh*—a mixture of tomatoes, cucumbers, cracked wheat, onions, olive oil and lemon juice served on shredded lettuce; and *dolmathes*—vine leaves that are stuffed with a rice mixture.

Diners sit at tables Western-style and use silverware to eat with. It is still advisable to eat only with the right hand so as not to offend or disgust anyone. Some of these restaurants also offer the option of sitting on cushions at a low table, Moroccan-style. If you

Left-Handed Diners

If you happen to be left-handed, it is fine for you to eat with your left hand. However, do not then get your right hand involved in the process.

select this option you may also need to request silverware. Waiters are politely out of earshot but are there to refill your water glass or fulfill a request at a signal from you. Seating is gender-mixed as is customary in Egypt, Lebanon and other non-Gulf Arab countries.

Foul Food

Foul (pronounced 'fool') is an Egyptian dish you may see on menus. It is a paste made of *fava* beans that is eaten with pita bread. Emiratis view it as a peasant's dish and as such hold it in contempt. If an Emirati asks you whether or not you eat *foul* he or she is teasing you. Laugh good-naturedly as it is meant in fun.

FINE DINING

Fine dining is available at hotels and shopping centres all over the UAE. Not a nation or type of cuisine is omitted. Some of the finest and most elegant dining is found in the Arabic/Lebanese restaurants and the Burj Al Arab provides the finest experience—quite possibly in the world. Also available: Chinese, Cuban, Egyptian, European, French, German, Indian, Italian, Japanese, Latin American, Malaysian, Mediterranean, Moroccan, Pakistani, Persian, Polynesian, Thai and Vietnamese.

THE ROADSIDE CAFÉ

Along with Lebanese restaurants, Indian restaurants are the most numerous. Lebanese restaurants tend to be more upscale and more expensive than the average Indian restaurant, but hotels do design elaborate Indian dining facilities and a high price to go with them.

The roadside cafés that one sees everywhere are, more often than not, places that serve Indian fare. They serve mainly spicy Indian cuisine and cater to the labourers. Some foods you might find in an Indian restaurant are *biryani*, which is chicken, mutton or fish cooked in mildly-spiced rice; and chicken or mutton *tikka*.

Dining in these restaurants is a cultural experience in itself. The restaurant is a simple room, usually having a dirt floor. Long metal tables fill the small room, with chairs or benches lined up around each table. The restaurant remains empty until the workers arrive en masse. Noisily they crowd the tables, and food is served in platters almost immediately, the same for everyone. All talking stops as the eating commences. The food, shovelled into the mouth with the right hand, disappears in minutes and one by one the workers rise, wash their hands and return to their jobs. These restaurants serve a sole purpose—that of eating. They are functional rather than pleasurable, set up to refuel the body as a gas station would refuel a car.

Slow Eaters

A girlfriend and I once stopped at one of these roadside cafés, seemingly in the middle of nowhere. It was about midday. We were seated at the end of one of the long metal tables on an earthen floor. We asked for a menu and silverware. Both took considerable time to be produced as the waiter had to go in search of them. We placed our order, and our food was served almost immediately. We dawdled over our food and were still eating at 1:00 pm when two trucks full of men pulled up and unloaded their human cargo. Men crowded in and managed to find seats everywhere but at our very long table. As they silently ate their meal, they stared unflinchingly at us like children seeing something for the first time. The meal done, the workers left immediately. It was curious to me that in a life of so few pleasures, one wouldn't linger a bit more over one's meal.

A MEAL IN THE PARK

Emiratis are proud of their parks which they refer to as gardens. They have them in every city, in particular in Al-Ain, which is also called the garden city. Some parks are for women only and most parks at least have women's hours when only women and children are allowed to use them. Emirati families can be seen in parks every evening and the foreign visitor is welcome too.

Some of these parks have restaurants with the usual fare described earlier under non-Gulf Arab cuisine. They feature an Arabic singer, or singers, and men get up from their tables and dance. The women, seated apart from the men in the family section, do not participate. It is truly pleasant to dine at these places surrounded by Arabic language and song, smells and ambience. You may want to try the 'hubbly bubbly', a fruit-

flavoured tobacco smoked from a large water pipe also known as *shisha* pipes. Be careful though, it is strong and will make you light-headed if you are not accustomed to smoking it.

WESTERN CUISINE

Hotels offer restaurants of every variety imaginable including Belgian, Swiss, Italian, French and Mexican. Also available are steak houses, tex-mex and chains such as Chili's and Planet Hollywood. You will be able to order cocktails, a bottle of wine to drink with your meal and an after dinner cognac if you so desire. The privilege will be reflected in your bill. Entertainment such as belly dancing or live music may also be part of your dining experience. The quality and variety of food are usually excellent. This is a great way to spend a date and the person doing the asking will usually do the paying as well.

Hotels are quite expensive with their prices and service fees. You can expect a service fee on everything, even on top of another service fee. Unfortunately price may not necessarily be reflected in quality of service. Frequently you pay five-star prices for three-star service. Be sure and complain. The UAE has a somewhat false economy, with a private sector going ballistic with its prices and a transitory expatriate clientele not sticking around long enough to keep things in check.

Numerous fast food places exist everywhere in Dubai and Abu Dhabi. Even Al-Ain sports a few. Food is usually ordered and picked up at the counter, though outlets such as Pizza Hut provide dine-in service. Often diners have the option of eating in the front room, where anyone may sit; or for women and families, in the family room, usually located upstairs.

The American tradition of 'going Dutch' where everyone pays for themselves is popular among many of the expatriates. The preference is to divide the bill evenly by the number of diners but there are still those who squabble over the last *dirham*. The Americans earn the stereotype for the squabbling and expatriates of other Western nations are known to limit socialising with them as a result. Of course, there are other acceptable forms of etiquette regarding the bill. One occurs in the pubs which follow the Irish and British custom of taking turns buying rounds. Reluctance to follow this tradition will not go unnoticed.

European-style coffee shops can be found everywhere. Some of these even have outdoor seating that is comfortable to sit at in the winter months. These cafés serve Arabic coffee, espresso drinks and regular black coffee; juices, sodas and mineral waters; vegetarian sandwiches and a variety of pastries.

ALCOHOL

Drinking is a major pastime for many of the single Western expatriates and Christian Arabs. Families tend to be more involved in activities children can participate in, but this is not a hard and fast rule. Organised activities frequently centre around or provide a reason for drinking. There are numerous night clubs in Abu Dhabi and Dubai and most of the other emirates have a couple. Thus many of the obvious means for meeting other Westerners centre around the consumption of alcohol. Alcohol is served in licensed restaurants and bars located

in hotels or sports clubs. Residents may obtain a liquor license to purchase alcohol in designated stores. A requirement of the license is that they declare themselves to be non-Muslims.

DISHES OF THE UAE

UAE cuisine is heavily influenced by Lebanese dishes. Typical ingredients are beef, lamb, chicken, seafood, rice, nuts (pistachios), dates, yoghurt and spices. Meals usually start with appetisers called *meze* and include pita bread and salad. The meal tends to be substantial and ends with a variety of desserts.

Some Typical Dishes

Spice, Rice and Noodles

- *Al Murr*: a spice used for stomach pains or treating burns.
- *Henna* leaf powder: used for dyeing and decorating hands and feet.
- *Bezar*: a mixture of local spices including cumin, fennel, cinnamon, coriander, pepper corns and dried chillies, and turmeric powder.
- *Ba-la-leet*: sweet vermicelli noodles with an omelette, both salty and sweet. It is served at any meal.

(Continued on the next page))

(Continued from previous page)

Spice, Rice and Noodles (continued)
- *Aash-ma-zaffran*: rice with saffron.
- *Ma-hammar*: sweet rice, a popular dish in the UAE made sweet by date syrup or caramelised sugar.
- *Ar-sea-ah*: chicken and rice paste, similar to cream of wheat. It is very popular when women visit in the afternoon.

Bread
- *Ba-theeth*: a date crumple originating in the UAE. This one is a favourite, especially with a cup of Arabian coffee.
- *Khameer*: meaning to leaven or ferment, this traditional Bedouin bread is served with cheese, eggs, chami, honey and home-made butter either for breakfast or dinner
- *Ra-gagg*: meaning thin and delicate, this is the most traditional of the UAE breads. It is made daily during Ramadan and is served with honey.
- *Ma-ha-lah*: meaning sweet, it is made in the same way as *ra-gagg* but with different ingredients. It is served with honey, eggs and cheese.

Fish, Chicken And Meat
- *Ya-reesh*: fish cooked with cracked wheat. The dish can also be made with chicken, and is usually only served during Ramadan.
- *Sa-mak koufta*: fish cakes, popular during Ramadan and afternoon visiting.
- *Sa-mak ma-ga-lee* (fried)/*bil fern* (baked)/*mash-wee* (barbecued): fish, an everyday dish.
- *Ro-be-yann nashif*: shrimp fried with spices. It can be made with meat or chicken.
- *Fa-reed*: chicken with bread served on its own, particularly during Ramadan to begin or break the fast.
- *De-jaj ta-ha-tah*: rice with chicken at the bottom. It can also be made with fish or meat. This modern local dish is common and very attractive. It is usually served with plain yoghurt, sliced limes and raw sliced onion.

(Continued on the next page)

(Continued from previous page)

Fish, Chicken And Meat (continued)

- *Sahh-naa* or *Ja-sha*: dried sardines ground with fennel.
- *Yar-yurr* or *Je-shed*: shark with spices, plentiful and reasonably priced at the market where it can be bought fresh. Fish at the market is generally taken to be cleaned at minimal cost. Buy a shark as long as your arm, and not longer or it will be tough. As in many cultures, shark is thought to make men strong and masculine.
- *Da-jaj murrag* or *saloona*: a traditional chicken stew made daily and served with steamed rice or *ra-gagg*. It is also a popular side dish accompanying fish or any main course. During Ramadan it is served with bread only and called *fa-reed*. It can be made with meat or fish.
- *Da-jaj mahshee*: stuffed chicken served on *ra-gagg*, the bread absorbs the juices and lends a flavour of its own. The dish is served hot with salad, lemon wedges and yoghurt. Also very good when made with lamb.
- *Matchboos* or *Fogga*: this dish can be made with fish, meat, chicken, shrimp or game and is always served with radishes, freshly sliced onion, sliced limes and dates.
- *Ha-rees*: a dish of meat, water and wheat. It is one of the most traditional dishes in the UAE and a favourite. Served to guests, at weddings, parties and Eid. During Ramadan huge portions of this dish are made to share with friends and neighbours, and is seen as an essential dish to break the fast. It can be made with meat, chicken or wild desert rabbit.
- *Kheema*: fried ground beef, an Indian dish which is quite popular in the UAE.

Dairy

- *Robe*: home-made yogurt, a traditional part of every meal. The locals believe it has healing properties. It is usually served in individual bowls at room temperature.
- *Laban*: fresh buttermilk. Bedouins typically drink it with every meal and pour it over rice to give the food a sharper flavour. Emiratis believe it helps with digestion, and is particularly appropriate to break the Ramadan fast.

(Continued on the next page)

(Continued from previous page)

Dairy (continued)

- *Haleeb na-gah*: camel's milk. It has a strong flavour and must be drunk slowly to allow the stomach to digest it. Served warm in winter, chilled in summer. It can be turned into cream or butter.
- *Chammi*: cottage cheese made by skimming the cream off fresh *laban*, then putting it into a churn made from animal skin.
- *Haleeb ma zaffran/hal/hal-balzan-ja-beel*: milk with saffron, cardamom, fenugreek or ginger.

Vegetables

- *Fig-aa* or *Zu-ba-dee*: wild desert truffles, found in desert areas of the UAE, amidst the bracken. They are usually found after the heavy winter rains, around March or April each year and are not easy to find.
- *Pa-ko-ra*: fried flour, vegetables and spices. These vegetable fritters were originally from India and are very popular in the UAE during Ramadan.
- *Samboosa*: fried savory triangle-shaped pastry can be filled with vegetable, chicken or meat mixtures. This dish also originates in India.
- *Fa-la-fel*: ground bread bean savouries, used as a sandwich filling. It may have originated in Lebanon or Egypt. Often eaten with *tahini*, a ground sesame seed paste.
- *Dhal*: an Indian dish of boiled lentils. It is very popular in the UAE.
- *Dnago* or *Nak-kee*: boiled chick peas.

Dessert

- *A-see-da*: browned flour pudding. Can be made with pumpkin.
- *Kham-fa-roush*: small fried rice cakes requiring minimal time to prepare. These are a great favourite during Ramadan.
- *Custard ma hall/loomi*: custard with cardamom or lemon.
- *Fir-nee*: ground rice pudding. This traditional, local recipe is a thick, rich dessert popular during Ramadan.
- *Sago man haleeb*: tapioca and milk pudding.
- *Le-ge-matt*: a traditional dough ball served with a sticky syrup.

(Continued on the next page)

(Continued from previous page)

Dessert (continued)

- *Cooz* or *peshew*: gelatine-flavoured custard, originally from Iran. It became a favourite in the UAE quite a long time ago before refrigeration was available. It does, however, taste better cold.
- *Um ali*: bread pudding, one of the best known desserts in the UAE. It is originally from Egypt but ingredients, of which there are many, have been adapted to those available locally. It is a favourite during Ramadan and means 'the queen of puddings'.

Drinks

- *Gah-wa*: traditional Gulf Arab coffee. It is made using fresh green coffee beans roasted in a frying pan over a direct fire, then pounded by hand in a mortar with a pestle until the beans reach a medium-sized grain. They are then boiled.
- *Aseer loomi ma bour-ta-gal*: fresh lemon and orange drink, usually served when visiting local homes.
- Various teas:
  Chai-jer-fau: cinnamon
  Chai zatar: thyme
  Chai-na'na: mint
  Chai zan-ja-beel: ginger
  Chai: plain

Forbidden Food

Muslims are forbidden to eat meat of an animal that has not been slaughtered in accordance with Islamic rituals (known as *halaal*). You will never see pork on an Arabic menu. This meat is taboo for Muslims—not just eating it, but preparing it or serving it. Do not offer it in your home when entertaining Muslim guests.

ENJOYING THE CULTURE

CHAPTER 7

'Eat whatever thou likest,
but dress as others do.'
—Arabic proverb

TRADITIONAL EMIRATI DRESS

In many countries, traditional dress is only on display at cultural events, but the UAE is unique in that traditional dress has remained as everyday wear for the Emiratis, dictated by climate and religion. The nationals maintain their traditional dress as a mark of social status and pride, and because it is extremely suitable for the climate. They discourage non-Emirati people from wearing it. Within their own social structure, their dress is made of finer materials with increasingly elaborate embroidery as their status rises.

The Qur'an encourages modesty in dress but does not require the extremely discreet garb worn by the Gulf Arabs. Dress is more a matter of custom. The Emiratis' religious belief is that the form of the body should not be apparent for men or women. They also believe in dressing very well in public. At home, more casual Western dress may be worn, even jeans. For a while many Emiratis were discarding their traditional dress for Western-style clothing, but the pendulum has swung back in the direction of conservatism and it is unusual to see the nationals in Western clothing, although they may do so when they leave the country on vacation or for business.

Men

Emirati men wear an ankle-length, loose-fitting white *kandoura* or *dishdash*. The gown has a high neck and long sleeves. On their heads they wear a skull cap called a *taquia* or *qahfa* and then cover this with a long, white cloth called a *gutra*. The two are secured by a wool rope called *al iqal* or *al ghizam* that is wound around the crown. The entire headdress protects the wearer from the hot sun. For ceremonies, officials and high-status individuals will also wear a flowing cloak trimmed with gold over their *dishdash* called a *thob* or *abba*. This garment is usually black, often with embroidery along the edges. Bedouin men also often wear a weapon, usually a *khanjar* which is a curved double-edged blade six to eight inches in length. The hilt is overlaid with silver and the scabbard is decorated with silver rings and wire.

Women

Emirati women wear a loose full-sleeved dress called a *kandoura*. This reaches to mid-calf and is heavily embroidered at the cuffs and collar. It has a round neck with a short slit down the front. Material used for the *kandoura* is often of colourful wool, cotton, and silk, brocade, satin or chiffon.

These gowns are worn by both older women as well as the younger generation. However, the younger generation has been influenced by high fashion runway styles. Blouses and long skirts commonly replace the simpler one-piece gown. These can be folded and tucked in numerous ways, have long flared hems and lacy sleeves, be covered with buttons, ropes and strings, and be complimented by platform shoes in the latest London style. Over this they wear a lightweight black cloak which is also often embroidered. This is called the *abaya*. For special occasions they will wear a *thaub*, a full-length loose overdress made out of chiffon and elaborately decorated. The *abaya* may cover the head; if not, a veil is worn, also of a lightweight black material and the *burqa*, made of coarse black silk with a central stiffened rib resting on the nose, covers the face.

The masks can be adornments that do not actually conceal much. They are worn to beautify and are cut to enhance a woman's positive features while hiding her blemishes. Especially-daring women cut their masks so that their upper lip is barely covered. The mask emphasises a woman's eyes

A Bedouin man with a *khanjar* knife strapped to his waist.

A group of Emirati women dressed in traditional black *abayas*.

and has probably contributed greatly to the exotic quality of eyes in Arabia. The covered parts of the face become another erogenous zone, covered except for intimate encounters.

Older women and married women wear a *burqa* that covers their eyebrows, nose and mouth. Exceptionally conservative women wear full-face masks. Cuts to the mask are made to the length and width of the eye slits. These masks are black and may have embroidered decorations on them. Women wear them comfortably and they become less intrusive as you grow accustomed to them. Older women who have worn *burqas* their whole lives have surprisingly few wrinkles. The

> The eyes tell a great deal. In my classes, about 20 per cent of the women were completely covered except for their eyes. I could pick those students out by name from a crowd of women as easily as I could those students only wearing a scarf.

current generation of young women seem to be discarding the mask, but there are still plenty of very traditional women who don the mask at puberty and remove it only for their husbands. A child whose mother wears the mask may never see his or her mother's face, but he or she would know her eyes and smell well enough to single her out. Because the eyes are seen, women accent them with kohl.

Women also wear henna on their hands and feet in intricate designs. Jewellery was their financial security so they wore it around their necks, wrists and ankles. In the past, silver was valuable and thus much of their jewellery were of silver with designs made out of valuable beads or coins. Now gold is the valuable metal and is found in gold *souks* everywhere. Traditional dress began to be worn again as a matter of prestige to distinguish 'free' women from slaves and now from hired help, many of who come from poorer Muslim countries.

THE MAJLIS

A *majlis* is a meeting or council in which members of a tribe can openly voice their opinions. The purpose of the *majlis* can be as simple as an informal social gathering or it can be to settle disputes. An area is dedicated in many homes and businesses for the *majlis*, and is an important defined space. It can be a tent or room in a house having wall to wall carpeting and large, firm pillows on the floor. Guests are met in this space and there may be separate spaces for men and women. A room,

Women And Children

The women gather in the *majlis* daily to gossip and to trade stories, jokes and medicinal remedies. Through the *majlis* talk, children learn the difference between right and wrong and how to bring honour rather than shame to the family.

however, is not required for the *majlis* to take place. The desert floor makes for a nice seat particularly if there is also shade nearby, and a seated group of men sharing a thermos of coffee on a roundabout at a fairly busy intersection of town is not an uncommon sight.

Anyone is welcome into a *majlis*, even the *majlis* of a ruler. The *majlis* was used in governance, which worked well for the Emiratis when their country was less populated and newly forming. The rulers would hold frequent and open *majlis* or councils to discuss the business of running the country.

As the country developed, grew in population and became more complex, the *majlis* as a source of governance has become difficult to maintain. With less direct access to their ruler on a daily basis, it has become more common for people to deal with government institutions relevant to their business.

THE MODERN EMIRATI

Most Emiratis now live in modern, single family dwellings. These may be palatial if the family is particularly wealthy. Their houses are often built around a courtyard so all rooms open into the central garden. The grounds are enclosed by high walls and a gate, making the once open tent-home of the desert a socially impenetrable fortress. However, the outer wall does serve the purpose of providing protection from the desert for the inner garden to grow.

Within the walls, some rooms are built as separate structures. The floors of the rooms are covered with Persian carpets, walls and ceilings are completely wall-papered, and there are pillows to sit on. There are chests, bookcases or low tables in some rooms but furniture in a Western sense does not feature prominently in their homes.

Emirati houses are equipped with electricity and running water. There may be several television sets, refrigerators, cookers (ovens) and washing machines in each house. Many of the Emiratis are wealthy to an astounding extent. Some own dozens of cars, wear Rolex watches, hire an army of servants, and have a palace in their hometown and also one in the vacation resort of Al-Ain or another Arab country. When a family member becomes seriously ill, that person may be flown to a hospital in London in a private leer jet to receive the best medical care money can buy. The family travels along and is catered to by the London staff.

The Emiratis can be annoying with their wealth. For example, some Emirati men carry multiple mobile telephones which they use quite remarkably all at once. The Emiratis, by the way, have very up-to-date communication systems; again, the best money can buy. From a Western perspective, these phones are more representative of toys rather than a useful and purposeful means of communicating. However, an Emirati's purpose in communicating is often to establish, confirm and reaffirm relationships. "Hello, how are you, how is your health, how is your father, how is your family?" is considered to be very purposeful communication to them.

Young men at the university may leave their four-wheel-drive vehicles running so that the air-conditioners can keep the truck cool while they attend their two-hour classes. Midway through the first hour their friends may call just to say hello. The Western male teacher may try to conduct class over the din of ringing telephones and students going and coming from the hall where they talk to the caller. The students respond to the teacher's frustration with, "No problem, Sir."

But this form of distraction is truly a problem and a huge source of frustration for the teacher, who places great importance on what he is doing and the time given him to accomplish his task. The conflict is with a time orientation, where the teacher has a plan for tomorrow and the day after tomorrow, all eventually culminating in the successful completion of the course. The Emiratis though are not future-oriented and are comfortable with learning or doing tomorrow whatever did not get accomplished today. Living in the UAE definitely requires a reorientation for time-bound Westerners.

TRADITIONAL GAMES

Games contributed towards the development of children's minds and bodies in preparation for adulthood in the harsh desert climate. Games for boys tested their strength and endurance, while girls played games that prepared them to run their future homes. These games not only reflected a history and struggle against the harsh environment, they also portrayed the culture and social structure of the tribe.

For example, *al-Boom*, a game with model boats is played by boys in which they come to understand their country's close relationship with the sea.

Falconry

Falconry is a sport in which the Emiratis train wild falcons to attack small prey and bring the prey back to serve as the evening meal. In the past, while this was every bit the valuable tradition and sport as it is today, it was also a means for the Emiratis to obtain fresh meat. The falcons' natural prey are wild rabbits, bustards, other birds, and small desert animals. Falcons can be bought at a market or trapped (using live pigeons as bait) as they migrate south. Skilful falconers tame their falcons with a gentle touch, rewarding them with food to train their behaviour. One end of a line is tied to a falcon's leg and the other end is held by the owner. The falcon is sent towards bait made of the wings of a bustard from a distance of 100 m or so. He is rewarded with a meal for attacking it. It is an art to train a falcon to be aggressive enough to attack a quarry, and at the same time be obedient enough to bring the quarry back to its master.

When not hunting, falcons can be seen perched on their owners' forearms. Special forearm guards are worn to protect the owners' arms from the falcon's talons. When at rest, the falcon's heads are covered with a leather hood to shut out movement which might startle them. The hoods keep the birds calm as if they had been sedated. Falconry is a winter sport beginning in October and ending in March when birds have migrated from Iran, Turkey, Russia and Syria. The falcons are released back into the wild at the end of the season.

Pearl Diving

Pearl diving was one of the UAE's primary income-generating industries before oil was discovered. Pearling vessels were made of wood and had one large sail. They anchored offshore, and men dove for oysters. A diver wore his undergarment and pinned his nose closed. A weight assisted his descent and he quickly dove six or more metres (20 or more feet) to the sea floor where he gathered oysters with his bare hands, placing them in a basket tied to a line held by another worker on the ship's deck. Each diver made about 50 dives a day lasting three minutes each. When he was ready to return to

the surface he tugged on the line and was hauled immediately to the surface. Sharks, sting rays and inattentive shipside partners all posed death threats to the divers.

The development of cultured pearl farms by the Japanese devastated the Emiratis' industry. General world demand for pearls was satisfied by the perfectly round and even pearls produced by the Japanese. Still, natural pearls like those found in the UAE are more valuable than cultured pearls, and the Emiratis' industry continues today on a smaller scale, and caters to the smaller market willing to pay a higher price for the real thing.

Fishing

Fishing was second to pearl diving in terms of income for the Emiratis. With over 100 km of coast line and 200 islands, coral beds supported a rich variety of life. Fishermen and their wives made cages out of palm leaves and nets to trap over a hundred different species of fish. The women salted and dried the fish or sold them at fish markets. Women also made the containers men used for collecting their catch, and these were made out of palm fronds. Skill in knowing where the best fish were to be found was critical, and a fisherman would pass his knowledge on to his sons, who would follow him in the trade.

Handcraft

Women used palm fronds to make many things, including circular mats to put food on, other mats for sitting upon, a cone-shaped mat to cover food and protect it from insects and dust, and fans to fan the fire, cool food, and to cool themselves. Bedouin tanned the skins of animals and used these in building houses and making buckets to draw water from the wells. They also made belts, shoes and clothing from the leather.

Pottery was made from a rich red clay found in the mountain areas. Some of these pots were clay incense burners the women decorated. Metals found were made into coffee pots, pots for cooking and pots for holding water and storing food items. Men used the metal also to make swords, daggers, spears and arrows. It was not unusual for the women to help in all these activities because tribal members were all part of a woman's incest group and it was perfectly acceptable for her to be around.

LEISURE ACTIVITIES

Sports is perhaps the number one alternative form of amusement for expatriates. Most expatriates exercise at a gym or join a team sport to alleviate boredom, even if they hate to exercise. Available competitive sports are rugby, softball, soccer and tennis, to name just a few. Adventure businesses abound and offer caving, scuba diving, rock climbing, camel riding, wind surfing and dune buggying. Also popular is racing: camels, horses, boats, and cars. There are a number of yacht clubs and golf courses which frequently hold international tournaments and award cash prizes. Green fees are exorbitant to cover the cost of maintaining grass in the desert.

The UAE is a premier golf destination with excellent weather and top-class facilities. Choose from numerous golf courses meeting international standards, or attend one of the many hosted and prestigious golf tournaments.

RUGBY'S THIRSTY WORK

COME ON KICK-OFF

TRIGO

Exploring the desert in four-wheel-drive vehicles is a favourite pastime of the Emiratis, particularly after rain when new *wadis* can be found.

For the nature enthusiast there is a natural history club, and if you get tired of listening to the lectures, your request to speak knowledgeably on a relevant topic will probably be met with enthusiasm. Many people purchase four-wheel-drive vehicles and spend a lot of time exploring the desert and *wadis,* or experimenting how much hard and adventurous driving their vehicles can withstand. If you do not have a four-wheel-drive vehicle, join a late afternoon tour group who will take you past camel farms to a sumptuous dinner at a traditional campsite. Hiking is excellent in inland areas. In the north, the Ru'us Al Jibal Mountains contain the highest peaks in the area at over 2,000 m. To the east are the very stark and beautiful Hajar Mountains which form the border between the UAE and Oman. Terrain is heavily eroded and crumbles easily, so be careful. There are easy walks to take in spectacular views or all day treks and major mountaineering on the faces of mountains.

Off the beaten track, there are many different classes offered and available time is just the thing for developing a new skill. Classes are offered in ballet, karate, belly dancing, horseback riding, ice skating and henna painting. Individuals offer private music lessons for piano, guitar and wind instruments. You can check the classified sections of one of the two major newspapers to find an instructor.

For expatriates who like their jobs (with higher salary and more time off) and have the right attitude, living in the UAE is a perpetual holiday. For others, the perks must constantly be weighed against the frustrations of daily life (the stares, traffic, the boredom, the different attitude towards time and multi-cultural contact).

Boat Cruises

Traditional dhows line the Dubai canal. Tourists may view the city from the comfort of a cruise that offers a pre-recorded commentary of Dubai's history. From this vantage point they gain a perspective on places of interest on land. Longer cruises are available and may include truly authentic Arabian dining. Some sites the visitor will see from this vantage point are the carefully restored Shindagha, the home of Sheikh Saeed who formerly ruled Dubai. A more modern site is the Creek Golf & Yacht Club which sports a golf course, marina and a landmark clubhouse on 200 acres of land on the banks of the creek.

The creek can be crossed on a small dhow called *abra,* meaning water taxi. These are incredibly inexpensive when one crowds in with the workers for the quick crossing. These smaller dhows can be contracted to provide a private tour up and down the creek for a price. More expensive evening dinner cruises are also available.

A tour along Abu Dhabi's waterfront is an opportunity to see the world's largest manmade port, the Petroleum Exhibition, Jebel Ali Free Zone, Al Husa Fort—the original home of the rulers of Abu Dhabi, and Abu Dhabi's magnificent corniche—a waterfront walkway spanning the length of the city.

Water Sports

Almost every imaginable water sport is available and makes for big business along with the promotion of the tourism industry. Many water sports are offered at the five-star hotels or private clubs at a high cost. Examples of these

Fishing here is an expensive activity since water in the creeks and close to shore is polluted, leaving deep sea fishing as the only option. Fish stocks have diminished, and so regulations have been introduced. You must either have a fishing permit, or join a chartered licensed tour guide.

are water-skiing, scuba diving, boat racing and fishing. Scuba diving and snorkelling off the Gulf of Oman near Shark Island is excellent because the water there is clear. Swimming in the Gulf is also a joy as the water is warm almost all year round. Water parks have been built with tubes, slides, caves and wave pools. Some hotels and a few independent operators even offer jet-skiing and parasailing.

Unusual And Unique Sports

There are no lack of the more unusual and unique sports and activities that you can enjoy in the UAE. These include:

- Organised safaris
  Organised safaris aboard camels or four-wheel-drive vehicles take tourists to a Bedouin campsite where guests can enjoy a barbeque dinner and belly dancing show. The belly dancing is not traditional to the UAE, but is very popular nonetheless.

- Ice skating/ice hockey
  There are several ice rinks in the UAE, and ice hockey is growing in popularity.

- Rollerblading
  Rollerblading is permitted on the corniche in Abu Dhabi, and at Jumeira Beach Corniche and in Creekside and Safa Parks in Dubai.

- Horse riding
  Dubai offers a world-class horse riding school which also boards horses.

- Sand boarding
  Sand boarding on a monoski, not unlike snowboarding, has evolved with boarders skiing down large sand dunes.

This requires either a hike to the top of a dune or a camel ride up as there are no ski lifts.

- Go-karting/racing
  You may go-kart for fun or compete regularly throughout the year. BMX and FMX riding are popular and Dubai hosts international competitions. Camel racing is a fascinating traditional sport. Races are held in winter on Wednesdays, Fridays, Saturdays and public holidays. Desert Rallies are organised throughout the year by the Emirates Motor Sports Federation, with the highest profile event being the UAE Desert Challenge, which attracts top rally drivers from all over the world.

- Powerboat racing
  Powerboat racing is growing in popularity, and the Dubai Creek provides a stunning setting for national racing events.

- Shooting
  Shooting is available indoors and outdoors. Practice targets are clay pigeons or real ones or can consist of laser guns in a simulation room.

- Flying
  Dubai offers many opportunities to fly. For as little as US$ 150, you can have a trial flying lesson and be a pilot for an hour. This is a fantastic way to see the marvellous development all around. You can also train for a private pilot's license, commercial pilot's license, instrument rating and multi-engine rating. Hot air balloons carry a dozen people over the city, mountains and deserts.

CALENDAR OF FESTIVALS AND HOLIDAYS
The Weekend

In 2006, the Federal Government changed the weekend schedule from Thursday and Friday to Friday and Saturday as the official weekend for all public sector establishments, government schools and universities. Many private businesses and schools have adjusted to this schedule, but not all have.

Calculating Holidays

Holidays are calculated using a mixture of official government announcements and predictive data. Holidays in the UAE are subject to arbitrary, last-minute changes by local authorities, and you should thus check with the UAE consulate or embassy before planning a trip. The casual tourist is advised to avoid Ramadan as society becomes more conservative and restrictive during that period, and hours of operation are subject to change for all businesses and tourist sites.

Religious holidays may vary from what was stated due to different interpretations between religious authorities or because it coincides with another holiday on a different calendar, or even because the day is deemed to be unlucky.

Many long-time residents of the UAE will schedule several flights out of the country around the anticipated time of the holiday. Once the start of the holiday is announced, they will cancel those flights that are too early and too late, and take the one closest to the announcement.

Lunar Calendar

The UAE follows the Islamic or Muslim calendar to determine the proper day on which to celebrate Islamic holy days. It is a lunar calendar of 12 lunar months totalling about 354 days.

Months of the Islamic Calendar

The 12 months of the Islamic Calendar are:

First month	MuHarram
Second month	Safar
Third month	Raby` al-awal
Fourth month	Raby` al-Thaany
Fifth month	Jumaada al-awal
Sixth month	Jumaada al-Thaany
Seventh month	Rajab
Eighth month	Sha`baan
Ninth month	RamaDHaan
Tenth month	Shawwal
Eleventh month	Thw al-Qi`dah
Twelfth month	Thw al-Hijjah

Construction is constantly taking place in the rapidly developing UAE. Here, an Asian labourer takes a seat opposite the construction site of the colossal Burj Dubai, an ongoing project that aims to become the world's tallest building upon completion. Its interior is to be decorated by Giogio Armani, who will also host the first ever Giorgio Armani hotel on the first 37 floors.

A group of fishermen pull in the day's catch at this beach in Ajman. With 36 km of coastline, fishing continues to be an important source of revenue for Ajman, the smallest of the federation of emirates.

Built by the Portuguese as early as the 16th century, the Bithna Fort in Fujairah is a historic landmark that once stood along a strategic route across the Hajar Mountains to fight off enemies and invaders.

The Dubai Air Show is held every year in November and attracts close to a thousand exhibitors from 50 countries. Here at this event, a Bedouin guard stands in front of the Airbus A380, one of the 45 that the UAE's national airline Emirates Air had purchased. With a 17.8 per cent increase in passengers in the first half of 2007, Emirates Air boasts the highest growth of any carrier in the world.

A wide variety of fruits and vegetables are available at this market in Fujairah. With a relatively high amount of rain falling on this mountainous and fertile region, Fujairah is suitable for agriculture as compared to its neighbouring emirates that experience a harsh desert climate.

Since the lunar year is about 11 days shorter than the solar year, Islamic holy days, although celebrated on fixed dates in their own calendar, shift 11 days earlier each successive solar year. Islamic years are called Hijra years because the first year was Prophet Muhammad's emigration from Mecca to Medina. Each number year is designated H or AH, in the year of the Hijra. The current Hijri Year corresponding to the Gregorian year of 2007 is 1428 AH.

Fixed Holidays

- 1 January
  This is the first day of the year in the Gregorian calendar. There are 364 days remaining until the end of the year (365 in leap years).

- 1 May
  May Day is celebrated on 1 May.

- 6 August
  This day marks the celebration of Sheikh Zayed's Accession to Presidency.

- 2 December
  National Day, Al-Eid Al Watani, is the celebration of independence from Britain in 1971.

Variable Holidays

- Islamic New Year
  The Islamic New Year, Ra's Al Sana Al Hijra, is celebrated on the first day of Muharram, the first month in the Islamic calendar. The estimated start dates for Muharram depend on sightings of the new moon, and strictly speaking the month starts at sunset on the previous day: 2008—29 December; 2009—18 December; 2010—7 December; 2011—26 November; and 2012—15 November.

- The Prophet's Birthday
  The Prophet's Birthday called Mawlid falls in the month

of Rabi' al-awal in the Islamic calendar. Sunni Muslims observe the holy day on the 12th of the month. Projected dates when Mawlid will be observed are: 2008—20 March; 2009—9 March; 2010—26 February; 2011—15 February; and 2012—4 February.

- Start of the Month of Ramadan
Eid al-Adha is a religious festival commemorating Ibrahim's (Abraham's) willingness to sacrifice his son, as commanded by God. It is one of two Eid festivals celebrated by Muslims, whose basis comes from the Quran. Eid al-Adha begins with a short prayer followed by a sermon. It is also called the "bigger" Eid because it is considered more important than Eid al-Fitr and it lasts one day longer. The dates of celebration are calculated to occur as follows: 2008—8 December; 2009—27 November; 2010—16 November; 2011—6 November; and 2012—26 October.

- The Night Journey
The Night Journey, al-Isra and Mi'raj, is the Prophet's Ascension, a two-part journey that Prophet Muhammad took in one night in AD 621 (1 BH). Many Muslims consider it a physical journey, but some Islamic scholars consider it a dream. The Prophet's journey begins in Mecca, continues to the "farthest mosque", considered to be the Noble Sanctuary (Temple Mount) in Jerusalem, and then to heaven where God tells the Prophet Muhammad to enjoin the Muslims to pray five times a day. The occasion is commemorated by Muslims in the UAE with long nights of prayer, sermons and reciting of the Qur'an in the mosques.

- End of Ramadan
The last day of the month of Ramadan, Eid al-Fitr, marks the end of Ramadan, the month of fasting, and is often abbreviated to Eid. Eid is an Arabic word meaning "festivity", while Fitr means "to break the fast" and so symbolises the breaking of the fasting period. The holiday is verified by the sighting of the new moon.

Muslims give money to the poor and wear their best clothes. Eid al-Fitr is a joyous occasion with important religious significance, celebrating the achievement of enhanced piety. It is a day of forgiveness, moral victory, peace of congregation, fellowship, brotherhood and unity. Muslims celebrate not only the end of all that fasting, but also thank God for the help and strength that they believe he gave them through the previous month to help them practise self-control.Eid al-Fitr lasts three days and is called "The Lesser Eid" compared with the Eid al-Adha that lasts four days and is called "The Greater Eid". On the Gregorian Calendar these dates are anticipated to occur as follows: 2008—somewhere between 2 and 5 October; 2009—21 September; 2010—10 September; 2011—August 31; and 2012—19 August.

LANGUAGE

CHAPTER 8

'Write the bad things that are done to you in sand,
but write the good things that happen to you
on a piece of marble.'
—Arabic proverb

ARABIC OR ENGLISH?

Arabic is the official language of the UAE and is used on all official documents. However, the conglomeration of so many people from differing nationalities and language backgrounds creates a need for a common language. The language chosen is the one spoken by the greatest number of people, and that language is English. Most highly placed officials or highly educated Emiratis are fluent in both English and Arabic, and switch back and forth between the two languages with ease and finesse.

Most non-national Arabs also speak both Arabic and English, and a large percentage of Eastern and subcontinent expatriates speak at least two languages—their native tongue and English or Arabic. Many shopkeepers speak three, four and more languages including English and Arabic in order to cater to the greatest possible number of customers. The monolingual groups tend to be the Western expatriates who are only able to speak English, and the nationals who only speak Arabic.

LEARNING ARABIC

For the native English speaker, learning Arabic is rather difficult. Arabic pronunciation is wildly different from English. Arabic contains many sounds not made in English that even with practice are difficult for the English speaker to produce. The most difficult of these sounds are those made at the back

of the mouth and throat (the glottals). Arabic is a stress-timed language making its rhythm predictable and regular, while English reduces and blends sounds together to fit its stress pattern. Intonation patterns of the two languages are used to convey meaning in similar ways; for example, both languages have rising intonation in questions.

Arabic grammar is markedly different from English. Verbs come before subjects and have particles added to them to change the sentence in various ways. Adding *laa* or *maa* to a verb makes it negative. Pronouns can be prefixed or suffixed to the verb, and still other particle additions are used to refer to the future. These particles are not only added to the beginnings and ends of words, but can be placed in the middle as well (called infixing). The verb is always gender specific, indicating whether the person speaking, the person being spoken to, and the person being spoken about are male or female.

Learning to read and write in Arabic is another hurdle, since the script is so different from English. Arabic letters are beautifully formed curves and lines bearing no resemblance to the Latin alphabet used in the English language. Arabic letters are written from right to left in cursive style with the letters within words connected to each other. A colleague had a student who wrote his English assignments from right to left, and she would hold them up to a mirror to correct them because despite her best efforts, a disability prevented him from learning to write left to right.

The Arabic alphabet has 28 letters, 22 consonants and six vowels. It has eight vowels and diphthongs, as compared to 22 vowels and diphthongs in English. There are three short vowels that are not written because they occur in predictable patterns so Arabs are able to read words even with these vowels missing. However, encoding words into script without these vowels causes confusion among readers and writers when script is being translated from English into Arabic. Your own name will be spelled and interpreted in translation any number of ways.

NUMBERS

English borrowed the Arabic numeral system of using one symbol each for 0 through 9, and adding new place values for tens, hundreds, thousands and so forth.

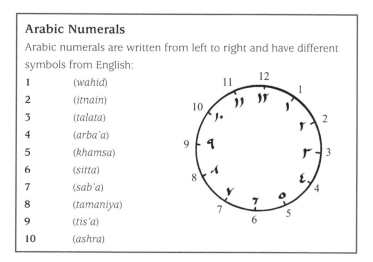

Arabic Numerals

Arabic numerals are written from left to right and have different symbols from English:

1	(wahid)
2	(itnain)
3	(talata)
4	(arba'a)
5	(khamsa)
6	(sitta)
7	(sab'a)
8	(tamaniya)
9	(tis'a)
10	(ashra)

CLASSICAL ARABIC AND DIALECT

As the Qur'an is written in classical Arabic, the Arabic language is thus considered sacred. It is used for all writing, for formal discussions and speeches and for news broadcasts.

Its grammar is more complex than that of any of the dialects, and 50 per cent of the vocabulary found in the Qur'an is not in everyday use. Few foreign words are incorporated into Arabic because Arabic has such a large vocabulary it makes coining new words easy.

People with a good command of classical Arabic are highly respected. This is equivalent to saying Arabs have a high respect for literacy, literacy being synonymous with classical Arabic. To foster literacy, substituting a written dialect might help, but there is great opposition to changing anything that comes from the Qur'an. A standard language helps to unite Arabs from so many nations and changing the standard would cause a linguistic splintering that would add to existing political and cultural differences.

Dialects are used in ordinary, everyday conversation and in films and plays. There are five dialects falling into groups by geography. Gulf Arabic is spoken by people from Saudi Arabia, Yemen, Kuwait, Bahrain, Qatar, Oman and the UAE. This dialect is intelligible to Arabs in Egypt, Sudan, Lebanon, Syria, Jordan and Palestine. However, the Iraqi and North African dialects are different enough to cause difficulty in comprehension. The main differences in dialects are in vocabulary. Arabs resort to classical Arabic when they don't understand each other.

The Best Language?

Arabs have an intense love for their language. They view their language as one of their greatest cultural achievements. This pride is felt only for classical Arabic and does not extend to the dialects. Arabs go to school to study classical Arabic but refuse to study their dialects, the languages in active use.

Language superiority is not an uncommon sentiment but Arabs claim they have proof of the superiority of Arabic. First of all, Muslims believe the Qur'an, which is written in classical Arabic, came directly from God. Classical Arabic, being the medium through which God chose to communicate, must therefore be superior to all other languages. They further claim its complex grammar lends itself to rhythm and rhyme, making it aesthetically pleasing to listen to when recited aloud.

TAKING LESSONS

Even though learning Arabic is difficult, it will certainly help you gain insight into the society and culture. The Arabs will be pleased and will regard you highly for trying and may even view you as something of a scholar. You must be highly motivated to learn the language in order to overcome the obstacles mentioned. Arabs are extremely flattered by efforts to learn their language. Your efforts, no matter how poor, will be met with appreciation and delight. Many Arabic expressions make reference to God and sound flowery when translated literally into English. They are commonly used in Arabic by foreigners in the UAE and even amongst one another.

> When taking lessons from Arabs, they will want to teach you classical Arabic because that is what, in their opinion, scholars study. The people I have known to attempt lessons in the UAE usually quit in frustration when they are unable to convince their teachers to teach them the local dialect.

LANGUAGE NEED

Language learning is greatly facilitated by need, and the biggest obstacle to learning Arabic in the UAE is that there is simply very little need for the English speaker to speak and understand Arabic. The Arabic that is needed tends to be suited to situations and includes a smattering of Urdu. Such situations tend to present themselves in taxis and shops that cater primarily to Arabs, where the shopkeeper is less likely to know English.

Some Arabic words having cultural or religious value are used hundreds of times a day. These are 'insha'allah' (God willing), 'mafi mooshcola' (It is no problem) and 'al hamdu lilah' (Thanks be to God). No matter how little of the language one does learn, these expressions become automatic for everyone. These expressions can be annoying, particularly insha'allah because it is said every time reference is made to the future. To the foreigner it feels like someone is saying, "Maybe, maybe not" when actually the Emirati means to agree that the event will happen but that it is entirely up to God. This leaves some degree of uncertainty and even suggests impropriety in being exact about the future.

Ritualistic greetings can last a very long time. These are annoying when they interrupt your very important business. An Emirati will answer the telephone or greet a friend or second customer as they enter the shop even though you may be speaking. Patience is called for those from cultures accustomed to giving and receiving undivided attention from an early age. Arabs and many of the labour populations have learned to participate in several conversations at once. The more you can participate in these interruptions (for example, greeting a newcomer) and understand that they are not personal snubs aimed at you, the easier it will be for you to go about your business.

The Place Of English

The Emiratis have realised their need to learn English. Dubai, being a major trading port, deals with people from all over the world and the Emiratis there must communicate in English. Abu Dhabi is the home of the government and sees ambassadors, diplomats and official visitors from all over the world. They have learned to communicate across their varied backgrounds through English.

The UAE sells most of its oil to Western, English-speaking countries. The country's white-collar workers all tend to be English speakers and communicate with one another in the language that is most comfortable to them. Even the Emirati policeman who responds to the scene of an accident may be faced with two English-speaking drivers, and be frustrated if he cannot speak a common language with them.

The Emiratis realise that the burden of language adjustment in an international environment is on them. While writing in English is difficult for Emiratis, they learn to speak English with relative ease and clarity. A lengthy oral tradition may contribute to their verbal linguistic adeptness.

Learning English

The Emiratis study English from grade school through college. They have difficulty learning English because of the great differences in the writing systems of the two languages. Another factor complicating learning is that Arabs write in a circular fashion, eventually arriving at the moral or point of a story; whereas Westerners and many native English speakers write in a linear fashion, getting directly to the point.

ARABIC AND THE QUR'AN

Because Arabic is the language of the Holy Qur'an, all Muslims, despite their nationality and location in the world, are at least a little familiar with it. People pay respect to written Arabic, believing that when no longer needed, the script should be properly disposed of so that the name Allah and quotations from the Qur'an never have the chance of landing on the ground, where they might be stepped on or used to wrap things. Arabs even carry written blessings and verses from the Qur'an in silver necklaces specially made for this purpose. These serve to ward off the 'evil eye' brought on by such things as envious looks.

Respecting The Qur'ans

Qur'ans are treated with much respect. They should be nicely displayed on the X-shaped wooden stands specifically made for this purpose or kept in their own velvet-lined boxes. One should never place anything on top of the Qur'an, put the Qur'an down on the floor, or keep it with other common books.

ARABIC AND ART

Arabic art is almost never representational because Islam prohibits the representation of living things in art. Artists

choose not to flout this tradition because they see reality as so beautiful, it would be futile to try and capture or copy it. Instead, Arabic art is decorative. As this did not leave the Arabs many avenues in which to express themselves, they became adept at constructing complex designs using plant patterns, geometric motifs and Arabic script.

Arabic script uses 12 basic signs to write its 28 letters, and these are then used with further variation to decorate objects such as bowls, dishes, book covers, door and window frames, as well as walls and domes of mosques. Verses from the Qur'an are usually used as the text in these pieces.

THE POWER OF WORDS

Arabs believe words have power, and that words can affect the outcome of events. To ensure a good outcome, Arabs will interject blessings for good fortune. Conversely, they believe swearing and using obscenities will bring misfortune. They do not swear, curse or cuss and are alarmed when others do, because they feel the speaker will bring evil to them. The direct and honest approach favoured by some nationalities may shock the Emirati. Positive words are favoured, and criticism is best kept to oneself.

> Arabs do not like to discuss anything bad such as illness or death since reference to bad things can make their outcome worse. Instead they use euphemisms, indirect expressions for something that might come across as harsh.

NON-VERBAL COMMUNICATION

Many non-verbal forms of communication are not physical and occur below the level of awareness. When intercultural differences are not perceived as "different", they are labelled instead as right and wrong, resulting in a negative judgment.

High-Context Culture

Arabs are generally from high-context cultures, in which meaning is embedded in context and dependent in large part on the listener understanding the speaker. Context that would explain meaning can be found in the environment or surroundings, the culture or the religion. Many expatriates, though, come from low-context cultures and expect meaning to be explicit in the words conveyed by the speaker. Arabs find such explicitness to demonstrate simplicity and are amused by lack of skill and creativity. They also find this style of communication to be quite direct, which may lead to a judgment of the speaker being rude.

Conversely, those accustomed to clear and direct communication may feel that an Emirati is beating around the bush, avoiding the point and being ambiguous. In being direct, the Westerner is striving for emotional neutrality or objectivity, but the ambiguity of an Arab speaker tends to evoke an emotional response from the Westerner.

Status Over Accomplishments

The Emiratis are a 'being' culture in contrast to Western 'doing' cultures. In Emirati culture, birth, family background, age and rank are very important. What or who an Emirati is carries far more importance than what he does. Western cultures on the other hand are focused on activity, and believe achievement and visible accomplishments are important. As a result, Westerners can be obsessed with measuring activity. This plays out in the language. When an Emirati is asked, "How are you doing?" he or she will likely respond with his or her physical or emotional well-being, and thank God for his blessings. Westerners may instead comment on activity, and mention how busy they have been, tell you where they have vacationed, or about a sport in which they are engaged.

Oral Tradition

As mentioned earlier, the Emiratis have an oral tradition. A story told is considered adequate evidence for a conclusion, and one person can represent the beliefs and ideals of an entire community. Westerners often have a literate tradition. They rely on facts and require evidence, reason and analysis. They see the Emirati approach as intuitive, subjective and worse, irrational. The Emiratis' oral tradition has given rise to great story-telling, thinking in images and non-linear thinking. They use multiple themes, talk about people and events and make tremendous use of symbols. Westerners tend to be linear in their thinking, expecting beginnings and endings to stories, focusing on objects and requiring empirical evidence. One thought leads logically and sequentially to another and is supported by evidence. Westerners may thus feel bombarded at processing the variety of images, themes and ideas presented by the Arab story-teller, and also frustrated that time is not segmented.

Functions Of Language

English speakers use language primarily to transfer information. Language is clear, objective, accurate, factual, linear, sequential and direct. A call for words is also a call to action (walk the walk, talk the talk). Speakers build an argument step by step. Conversely, Emiratis use language to create a social experience. Language stresses on emotions, and to do so engages the use of melodious sounds, plays on words, recitation of the Qu'ran, prose and poetry. Poets are highly esteemed for their skill with language, and it is the language of Arabic itself for all these reasons that has become a symbol of Arab nationalism as it is for art and religion. The oral nature of the language prevents the speaker from being separate from their message or their audience. The oral nature of the language requires an audience, in keeping with the collective or group nature of the Emirati culture. Reading and writing on the other hand are singular activities, and in keeping with Western individualism.

Eye-Contact

Prolonged eye-contact is perceived as showing an interest in another person and the conversation. Emiratis also use it to help them gauge the truthfulness of the other person, and someone who does not maintain eye contact is seen as untrustworthy. Western cultures do not sustain eye contact as long and may find this to be uncomfortable.

Odours

The Emiratis are comfortable with natural body odours, seeing them as normal. They are favourably inclined to many aromas Westerners might find to be strong, such as the incense Emiratis frequently use to perfume themselves.

Persuasion

Emiratis favour repetition. They may be wordy, or repeat something over and over again. Westerners may thus be mistaken that an Emirati thinks he or she was not heard, or was not taken seriously.

An Emirati will often use imagery, as well as adjectives and adverbs to engage the listener. These metaphors may seem outlandish to a Westerner who would likely use facts and figures to illustrate the same point. For the Westerner, less is more and they will understate an event for emphasis.

Emiratis favour exaggeration, and overstatements may seem extreme or violent to Westerners. A persistent American stereotype of Arabs is that they are violent, boastful and insincere, when in fact, the truth may lie in a difference in styles of communication. This is further exacerbated by the tendency, particularly in American culture, to tie words to action. Words and actions are very far apart in Arab culture, which tends to discuss and negotiate issues at great length without action being taken. As a result, stereotypes of laziness and dishonesty may be attributed to the Emiratis.

Much can be learned from the Arab's skill and emphasis on words. Out of these different styles of communication, the most valuable awareness can come from understanding language as a social lubricant and tool for promoting social harmony among the Emiratis. Avoid direct questions when answers could lead to a loss of face, and be appreciative when your own has been spared.

WORKING AND DOING BUSINESS

CHAPTER 9

'Dig a well then close the well,
but do not unemploy a worker.'
—Arabic proverb

ECONOMICS

In 2005, the UAE came out of a 20-year period of deficits and posted a US$ 10 billion surplus. The strong oil market was a key contributor to the year's gains as were local stock markets, public-private ventures, private property developments, building and construction, and government investment in education, health and social services, transportation and communications. Growth in diversified sectors has reduced the country's dependence on oil revenues from three-quarters to one-third, and the country's growth is enabling it to invest in advanced technologies.

The government has increased spending on job creation and infrastructure expansion. It adheres to a strategy of economic diversification through the introduction of new productive sectors. This strategy and revenue from foreign investment has somewhat immunised the economy to fluctuating oil prices. The Emiratis consistently maintain a surplus in trade balances. Other government policies to diversify income resources and lessen dependence on oil as the sole source of revenues have also been effective.

Abu Dhabi is the largest and wealthiest emirate, and it has the largest population. As such, it dominates the federation. Abu Dhabi desires strong integration of the seven emirates, while the other six emirates wish to retain some degree of independence and autonomy. At the same time, they do not wish to lose the financial generosity of Abu Dhabi. Dubai is second in size, wealth and population among the emirates. It has fought hardest to retain as much independence as possible and, along with Ras Al Khaimah, is not entirely federally integrated. In addition to oil revenues, Dubai gets revenue from its trading industry. Tourism is the third main revenue-producing industry and again affects Abu Dhabi and Dubai more than the other emirates. The other emirates do not have the economic growth of Abu Dhabi and Dubai; they are also not as subject to social change. Westerners desiring more interaction with the local culture and an authentic experience will want to consider finding work in these emirates.

INFLATION

Inflation is running at record highs in the UAE, driven primarily by surging housing costs. The UAE is limited in its ability to control inflation because the *dirham* is pegged to the US dollar and the UAE must follow US monetary policy, which has the US Federal Reserve cutting interest rates. When the US lowers its deposit rate, the UAE follows suit and this constrains their central bank's efforts to contain inflation. Talk emerged about floating the *dirham* but this is unlikely to happen as it would cause a decrease in income in the oil sector. In 2006 the government imposed caps on rent increases and has considered other price controls to check inflation. Possible controls could be achieved through ceilings or limits for lending to high growth sectors and by adjusting salaries. Also in progress are laws, including real estate market regulation and regulating the production and distribution of goods.

Economic benefits Westerners receive sometimes decrease as the numbers of workers seeking jobs in the UAE increase. Of course, the people most hurt by inflation are those least able to cope with it—the labour population.

The UAE still has one of the highest per capita incomes in the world. Western expatriates earn healthy tax-free incomes, often with rent-free accommodation and airfare home once or twice a year. While incomes are still healthy, inflation has eroded that for many expatriates.

TOURISM

A major new sector that the UAE has been expanding is tourism. In 2005, tourism represented 1.2 per cent of Abu Dhabi's total GDP, and the emirate received 1.2 million visitors. For Dubai, which saw 6.1 million visitors arrive the same year, the tourism industry represents 30 per cent of its economy. Dubai has a goal of increasing its economic growth by 11 per cent a year and reaching a GDP of US$112 billion by 2015, with tourism being key to achieving that. Tourism is becoming increasingly important to all seven emirates, and they are well on schedule to achieve growth targets.

FutureBrand releases an annual report on how citizens and the rest of the world perceive a country. In 2007 the report was favourable to the UAE, citing the country as a 'rising star'. The UAE was ranked first for having the largest number of new properties and greatest variety of accommodation, from family style to seven-star hotels. It ranked second as a shopping destination behind the US, fifth as an excellent place to hold conferences, and seventh for fine dining. The

In 1992, when I mentioned to people that I was headed to the UAE, they would often ask, "Where exactly is that?" I almost never get that question anymore. Instead, they are more likely to respond, "Do you mean Dubai?"

UAE is listed in the report as 'UAE (Dubai)' because many people are mistaken that the country is Dubai, unaware of all the other things to see and partake of outside this one well-marketed city. This is most unfortunate politically, and many foreigners perceive Dubai as a brash city and not an ideal place for an authentic holiday. Abu Dhabi, on the other hand, is pitching itself as a repository for culture, the arts, and for its attractive architecture. Because of its greater size and methodical planning, Abu Dhabi will quietly and steadily gain worldwide awareness, and this will likely in turn promote the beauty of the smaller and lesser-known emirates as well.

Simply The Best

The Emiratis are on a superlative bandwagon. They boasts the tallest building in the Middle East (Dubai Trade Centre); the world's largest man-made port (Jebel Ali Port); the freest trade; and they are doing their best to attract big sporting events, such as the golfing PGA European circuit includes the greens of Dubai on its rounds and the annual Dubai Offshore Powerboat Race to name a few. The UAE may be young as a country, but it is sharp and quick to improve on new developments in the world. The country's officials purchase full page ads in foreign papers advertising their duty-free shops and encourage people to come and do business. They publish and market books with large colour photographs and flattering words about the country, and they have cultural centres in foreign cities to further promote the country and culture.

Growing Pains

Visitors come to the UAE every year to partake of the wonderfully mild winter; experience a setting remarkably different from their own and shop in the numerous marketplaces. However, developing tourism forces a conservative Muslim people to allow alcohol consumption, religious and racial freedom, and adopt English as the unofficial common language in their own country. Social freedom has also forced the Emiratis to face such problems as prostitution, drug smuggling and illegal immigration, to name a few. Another new source of income the country seeks is the imposing of tariffs and taxes, where none existed before. Emiratis themselves are exempt from these tariffs and taxes, while the foreign population would be detrimentally affected. The expatriate population feels anxious about these pending tariffs.

> While the Emiratis allow a liberal lifestyle in their country, they do not allow it for themselves. Severe punishment is meted out to the Muslim, regardless of nationality, who breaks the laws of Islam.

BEYOND THE OIL BOOM

Growth resulting from increased oil production has stopped, and the emirates are maintaining their current output level. Even though the economy has slowed down since the great oil boom, the UAE is still in an expansion stage. For years I have been listening to foreigners predicting that its growth would have to stop soon, but it hasn't, and opportunities for doing business in the UAE still abound. People are constantly coming and going, resulting in turnovers and vacancies. The service industry is ever expanding to support growth in the trade and construction businesses. Repair and maintenance work are lucrative businesses (due to shoddy workmanship up front and the harsh climate), managers with education and experience are always in demand to oversee it all. Asia is becoming interested in the Middle East for not just its oil, but also for the work opportunities and the wonderful climate. This market has barely begun to be tapped.

INTERNATIONAL RELATIONS

The UAE enjoys good political and economic relations with the European Union and Asian countries. It also has strong trade ties with the US. In fact, the UAE is the US' largest export market in the Middle East, and 750 American companies have a presence in the country. Throughout its growth as a nation, the UAE has generated most of its oil revenues from sales in Asia, which it then invested in the US economy.

The UAE has a long-standing tradition of diplomacy. In a region torn by strife, the country avoids conflict and maintains neutrality. The UAE is in favour of a nuclear weapon-free Gulf, and has appealed directly to Iran on this issue. While it opposes the US invasion of Iraq, it does support the US' commitment to stabilise the country and to establish a fair and inclusive political system engaging all Iraqis. The UAE also supports a peaceful, two-state resolution in Palestine.

The UAE is closely aligned with the US in its strategic interests, with reliable energy supplies, free trade and investment as well as a terrorist-free region being the common desires of both nations.

Stability and security in the Gulf are critical to the UAE's sustained economic success. To this end, the UAE cooperates with the US by allowing the US military to use its ports and locate troops within its boundaries. The UAE further offers law enforcement cooperation to help control the illegal flow of money, and to monitor sensitive shipments of containers through its ports.

Defence Spending

In accordance with the 1996–2005 rearmament procurement, the UAE has US$ 15 billion to spend on defence. By buying planes under a commercial sales agreement, the UAE is able to work around the US Defense Department's 2.5 per cent levy on foreign military purchases. This is just one of the special privileges the UAE has in defence dealings with the US.

BUSINESS OPPORTUNITIES

The UAE offers an abundance of business opportunities in different industries. Major imports include machinery and equipment, cars, aircraft, textiles and chemicals.

Telecommunications

Telecommunications has been a strong industry for the UAE for many years. Etisalat is the UAE's primary telephone company and now, after laying a network with US-provided routers, the company offers nationwide broadband services.

Internet penetration is higher in the UAE than anywhere else in the Arab world. It also has the highest rate of growth in the world, and this growth is expected to continue.

US company Hughes Space and Communications International, in collaboration with the UAE's Thuraya Telecommunications, manufactured, launched and provided ground facilities for two high-powered telecommunications satellites. These satellites service more than one-third of the world's population. Du is the name of the newest telecommunications provider, and it should provide competition for Etisalat, although prices have yet to drop.

Development Projects

The UAE is working to increase its power and water supplies to avoid shortages as demand continues to grow at a rate of 10 per cent each year. Companies specialising in power production, desalination and water purification should find ample opportunities in the UAE.

Abu Dhabi and Dubai are planning and preparing for population growth with the development of high-rise buildings, new hotels and the expansion of airports. This will open up opportunities for companies that supply heavy equipment and building products.

Companies providing pollution control equipment are in demand, in response to a 1999 federal environmental law protecting the environment. Both the government, through the Ministry of Health, and the private sector are adding new hospitals to cope with the increasing demand on the health care system.

The UAE continues to expand its production of gas and oil. This should ensure the healthy growth of the construction and engineering industries.

Small Business Owners

Foreigners with their own businesses are usually involved in the import-export sector, or are professionals in independent practice. With a few exceptions (as discussed later), business owners are required to have a national as a sponsor or business partner. Oil and gas exports account for the largest

There is supposed to be a tariff on goods in the UAE, but over half the goods come in and go out duty free. Items that are watched more closely and definitely taxed upon are alcohol, weapons and chemical substances, with alcohol and tobacco products incurring a 30 per cent tax. Drugs, pornography and anti-Islamic literature are entirely illegal.

portion of the export business at an estimated 75 per cent.

The UAE is also a place to buy products reasonably cheaply and to resell them at home for 150 to 200 times as much. These products come from Japan, South Korea, China, the UK and the US, and are re-exported at profit. The re-export trade has existed in the emirates ever since traders first began landing their boats on the coast. Opportunities for making money in the re-export business constantly shift with global political and economic conditions. Currently the Russians are shipping electronics out in huge quantities. It is actually astonishing to behold. Perhaps a dozen people fly in on a full size aircraft. They shop and play for a week or only a weekend, load their goods aboard the aircraft carved out to hold the goods and few passengers and head home to sell their wares on the black market. Many ports around the world can complain about the same phenomena at this time, but it is doubtful whether any are so blatantly obvious as the ports in Dubai and Sharjah.

UAE's Re-export Trade

The UAE is an international transport hub. Merchandise is imported and exported with a mark-up and with low or no taxes. The UAE's geographic location is excellent for moving goods quickly in response to demand, the transport system is superb probably because it was established centuries ago. The volume of trade helps pool risk so goods purchased from a large number of producers are repackaged and distributed across many markets. The UAE is able to deal in volume and circumvent trade barriers by disguising the country of origin. Firms are also able to transfer profits from high tariff places to the UAE by shipping to the UAE at an artificially low price and then marking up the goods significantly before they are re-exported to yet another place. Characteristic of transport hubs, the UAE has little in the way of manufacturing, but does have simple processing such as sorting, and packaging and service activities such as marketing.

Small business owners in the UAE are able to benefit from the tax-free environment and liberal trading regulations.

Foreign professionals running their own businesses include medical doctors, psychiatrists, psychologists, dentists, lawyers and other service providers. They are unique in their professions in that they need to be familiar with the Arab culture and language, and they tend to do well financially.

CONDUCTING YOUR BUSINESS
Personal Contacts

Contacts are vital in doing business here, as they are in most places. These contacts will inform you of forthcoming projects before they are announced. Knowing the right people, and getting along with the Arabs, will ensure jobs go to you over other bidders.

Success in business is more likely if you are personally around to conduct your operations, as your physical presence is preferable to letters and faxes from home. If you cannot be present yourself, you will need a representative or agent on a temporary (project) or permanent basis, depending on the nature of your business.

As your business expands, the agent may appoint sub-agents, or you may hire other agents for other emirates. Your agent, being the one with the contacts in the country, is in a better position to appoint other trusted and well-connected people as agents than you are, so you are probably better off giving him or her the reins. Care needs to be taken in selecting an agent, because while removing them is theoretically possible, in reality they cannot be removed or changed once in place.

Wasta

In a country where nepotism is prevalent, having established clout, or *wasta*, with a person in command is your only way in. This clout results in greater efficiency in getting your work done and fewer stumbling blocks.

Getting your foot in the door is difficult when you do not know anybody. *Wasta* refers to the connections and the pull a person has. This force was once used to resolve tribal conflict, but it has evolved into acquiring economic benefits. Whereas people once helped others for prestige, they now seek monetary rewards. This means you can often purchase the privileges you seek. A good attitude, acceptance of the local customs and conforming to local standards and customs are also keys to success and building the pull and connections that will get you further. Make friends among well-connected people and important, highly placed Emiratis. They can send business your way. At work, your advancement may proceed faster and further once you do get in if you are willing to put in the time on the job, and if you adapt to Emirati ways. Expect delays, frustrations and inconveniences and get the job done nevertheless.

Interpersonal Communication

Always consider a person's 'face' when communicating, including your own. Calm, controlled, unemotional speech is most appropriate. Patience and quiet insistence may not move you any closer to your goal than loud and forceful speech, but you will come out ahead in the future in not having lost respect among the Arabs. They may be more willing to say yes the next time you submit a request.

Saying No

'No' should be prefaced and softened, because saying it directly is offensive. You should be busy or offer some other reason why granting the request is not possible. Offer assistance at another time to further mitigate your refusal.

Similarly, in dealing with an employee who is not meeting your expectations, compliment the employee on what he or she is doing well, enquire about the health of the employee and their family (but do not enquire about the women), and explain how you would like to see things done in the future. A more direct approach will surely be taken as a personal attack, causing the employee to lose face and further encouraging the behaviour opposite from which you had hoped for. Do not ask an employee to do a job belonging to someone else, and never reprimand an employee in front of other people.

The Emiratis are open and sincere in communicating their wishes. While they do engage in ritualistic talk prior to discussing business, one does not have to decipher or second-guess their meaning as they are inclined to state it directly. They look you in the eye when speaking and expect you to do the same. Looking down or away is interpreted as dishonesty. Emiratis may ask you a slew of questions you may consider to be personal. These may be about your family, age or income. It is important to them that you feel at ease and at home as a guest in their country and their business environment. Establishing a personal relationship

with someone is a necessary precursor to establishing a business relationship. The more you warm up to them and they to you, the further your business will go.

Dressing And Manners

Emiratis typically see Westerners in particular as being too liberal and sloppy about their appearance. The Emiratis in general are immaculate dressers. Their clothes are well-pressed and elegant in a subtly expensive way. Your dress reflects your status and wealth, and you will be judged by your appearance. Your employers may also implement a dress code. Dress well—a couple of very nice, conservative outfits should suffice in the beginning.

Manners must be as impeccable as dressing. The best mannered people get the job. These people are the ones who let the Emirati set the pace, follow his lead in introducing business, and are sensitive to the amount of time the Emirati has or wants to devote to them. They wait for the Emirati to present his business card before offering theirs. Foreigners are forgiven for most of their strange ways, particularly when their intentions are well-meant. Openness needs to be tempered and subdued. If you cannot appear to be calm and relaxed, you should return when you are better able to master your feelings of anger and frustration or excitement and exuberance. Avoid insulting or shocking the Emiratis, and try to be non-judgmental.

Etiquette

Men should always shake hands with other men when meeting them for the first time. A handshake should be short and firm. Your first question should be, "How are you?" followed by, "How is business?" and then, "How was your vacation?" or, "Did you have a nice weekend?" and anything else you can come up with of a not-too-personal nature.

If a woman offers her hand, shake it, but do not put her in the awkward position of having to refuse your proffered hand because it is against her religious beliefs to touch you.

To Shake Or Not To Shake?

In general, people accept that foreign women shake hands with both men and women. However, I have been soundly rebuked for offering my hand to a Muslim man. For awhile I had travelled extensively between Asia, the UAE and the US, and it was indeed difficult to remember when to kiss, when to bow and when to shake hands!

Work Attitudes

Attitudes toward work are as varied as the population. People actually involved in business really do work hard. Expatriates in the private sector work a five-and-a-half-day week. Hours are long though, so for many people, this usually equates to a six-day work week. On the other hand, people who work for the government or ministries (usually Emiratis and diplomats) work a four-and-a-half-day week, with rarely any overtime. Their jobs are secure and their attitude towards work is very relaxed compared to the small business person who is trying to keep his or her company afloat.

Among the Emiratis, work attitudes also vary. The stereotypical Emirati businessman is a government official, royalty and sideline businessman all rolled into one. He is so highly placed, he must attend one formal engagement after another. Work attitudes are more relaxed in the UAE than they are in many other countries. This is evidenced by the common phrases: 'insha'allah' (God willing), 'ma'alish' (Don't worry) and 'mafi mooshcola' (No problem), indicating time is less important than being, relationships, and God. Emiratis do not usually become overburdened by all their responsibilities as might be expected. Added responsibility does not increase the pace because there is always tomorrow to do the work, and if it does not get done, well, that was God's will and out of one's control.

Discussing Business

The Emirati businessman you need to talk to is probably busy. He may have several businesses of his own, and serve as the chair for a half dozen or so committees and government offices. Other people need to see him too. Thus, his office will often be crowded and he will be conducting

When meeting an Emirati businessman in his office, you may enter a room full of people waiting for their business to be attended to by the one man behind the big desk. Greet him, shake his hand, sit down as close to him as possible. He will probably attend to you fairly quickly out of curiosity if you are a Westerner, since he normally sees fewer Westerners as compared to Middle and Far Easterners. Women usually do not have long to wait at all.

business with several people at once while signing official documents. All activity stops when a newcomer arrives (except for the tea boy) and he is greeted by those already present. Anybody present can and will offer their own perspective on the business being discussed at any given moment. You may feel largely ignored—have patience, you will be attended to.

If your business is sensitive, you may be asked to return at another time or be taken into another room where the door will be locked. A busy associate may get down to business rather quickly, as he is too caught up to spend much time coddling you. He will still ask ritualistic questions,but probably fewer of them, and he will be less attentive to responses. Follow his lead and state your business when asked for it clearly and succinctly, without leaving out important details. Avoid complicating your request.

DIRTY HANDS

A large percentage of the working population are adverse to doing anything outside of their job description, particularly if they feel it is beneath them, and even more so if the work involves manual labour. This is the 'dirty hands' concept and it results in a larger number of employees supervising work rather than actually doing the work—too many chiefs, not enough Indians. Furthermore, doing work that is beneath a person's position is demeaning. A hard worker who wants to start a business should adopt a similar 'dirty hands' concept with the public, then perform the work in private and reap a handsome profit.

The importance of prestige cannot be overemphasised in a country where six of its seven leaders can boast of having an international airport and three of them a daily newspaper. A private office is a sign of prestige. As an owner, manager or supervisor you will need your own office even if that is not your style. Psychologically, others will prefer to do business with such an important person as you, a person far removed from having dirty hands.

EMIRATIZATION OF JOBS

There is a concerted push to hire nationals over expatriates in government and business positions, particularly for positions that are unrelated to manual labour. Contacts and *wasta* will certainly assist in the hiring practice. Emirati men are assigned positions based on who they know. They often hold several government positions or commissions at one time.

Nepotism, while as widely practised as ever, has become less of a problem than in the past, now that most young nationals have good educations (many have college or university degrees, which are often earned abroad). It is thus likely that quality and productivity will accompany the relative that is handed the job. At least the potential is there. Educated Emiratis have made it possible for the UAE to grow into a mature participant in the business world. With this maturity has come the desire and ability to take over businesses and developments from foreigners.

The UAE government reports the number of jobless nationals as follows: 8,000 in 1995; 24,000 in 1999; 30,000 in 2003; and 35,000 in 2005. These unemployment figures continue to increase.

Still, unemployment among nationals is a problem. Rapid development over the past two decades in light of the abundance of natural resources has reduced the incentive to work because of non-wage income (social spending, dividends and low taxes). The UAE passed through major economic and social changes during the boom of the 1970s and early 1980s, followed by a bust in the late 1980s and 1990s. The rulers used the economic gains to implement a generous welfare system and served as the first place of employment. This overcrowded the public sector and placed a burden on the government to provide salary and benefits packages, that in addition to pensions included subsidised housing, schooling and health care. This clustered the nationals into a single sector and resulted in the widespread underemployment the Emiratis are experiencing now. In addition to expectations of high wages, the Emiratis expect minimum production and plenty of leisure hours. The UAE further opened its borders to foreign workers to ensure abundant labour at competitive wages, and this further segmented the labour market. As the Emirati's expectations are too high for the low-skill, low-wage jobs that the private sector generates, many nationals remain unemployed as a result.

The Ministry of Labour (MOL) is focused on resolving the unemployment problem among UAE nationals by recruiting nationals to all government establishments. They are promoting teaching programmes, and training and rehabilitating unsolicited, non-employed specialisations in the labour market to transform them into wanted specialisations. One thing the UAE government would like to see is for the private sector to offer 1 per cent of jobs annually to nationals. This is a real challenge when a foreigner can be found with eight years more in experience and is willing to work for 135 per cent less in wages. National hires are seldom successful because of the unrealistic expectations of the nationals.

The UAE government is investing heavily in improving the country's educational system through partnerships with the best universities around the world and providing on-the-job training. They are also striving to implement effective training programmes to help the nationals bridge the experience gap in a relatively short period of time. The UAE's banking sector is one small but significant area of success, employing nearly 30,000 Emiratis, which represents over 30 per cent of labour in the sector. This is important because the sector serves as a stepping stone for nationals to move into other industries.

ENTRY-LEVEL JOBS

Entry-level positions, such as secretaries, office workers or shopkeepers are advertised in the newspapers. Agencies requesting and supplying temporary help dominate the recruitment ads. These jobs do not usually offer benefits or a working visa, and pay about 5,000 dhs a month (US$ 1,358), almost enough for a single person to live on. The ads do not mince their words. They state exactly what they are looking for, including the gender, age, skin colour, accent and languages spoken.

Secretarial, office and shop staff jobs do not often come with opportunities for advancement anywhere, and this is also true in the UAE. There is a lot of lateral mobility at this level because employees change jobs when they receive a better offer. People who typically fill these positions are wives who do not have to worry about getting a work visa, Western women from GCC countries whose passports allow them to stay in the UAE for three to six months without a visa, and people from poorer countries where comparable job salaries are much lower.

JOB NEGOTIATION

It is difficult to know ahead of time whether the salary and benefits package you are being offered will be competitive in the UAE. You do not want to ruin your chances at a job by asking for more than the market offers, yet you will be disillusioned if you discover you have accepted a lower salary than your colleagues. You may feel you have undersold yourself, while your Arab employer is feeling good about the bargain he got. Never mind that you may be a disgruntled employee and will cost him in turnover in the long run, he is pleased with his deal at the present time.

There are no set answers but a little advice will help one get on the right track. Get as much information as you can from prospective employers. If they are above board and reputable, they will supply you with satisfactory answers. Be careful if a benefit you want is not in your contract, for it will not be forthcoming after you arrive. If you want something, ask upfront.

One pitfall that may lead to job dissatisfaction is that while you will probably be given annual cost of living adjustments (which may or may not keep up with inflation), raises are less likely. This is one way the Emiratis discourage people from staying in the country too long. If you are interested in annual reviews resulting in pay increases, you should get it in writing up front. A person's word is purported to be more important than a written contract. With large organisations, the contract serves as the spoken word, and with one's word goes honour, so it will be followed.

WESTERN WORKING WOMEN

Surprisingly, professional working women will find themselves treated with an equality and respect at work that is perhaps superior to their experience in the West. Colleagues, male and female, take their opinions seriously and women are as likely to be promoted as men. Equal compensation is even given for comparable work. The UAE is a veritable paradise for women seeking an equal voice and equal opportunities at work.

Having a relatively small population gives women (or everyone for that matter) the opportunity to start businesses or carry out other endeavours. Thus, Western women are often active in establishing businesses, professional organisations and clubs. In the UAE, the time, funds and facilities are available to achieve such goals.

However, secretarial and retail positions are often subject to the same discrimination, harassment, tedium and lack of respect as they are in the home country. They might be a little more interesting in the UAE because of the cultural variety, but this may also cause them to be more frustrating as well. While these positions do pay a little better than they would at home, the cost of living in the UAE might be significantly higher.

TAXES

There are no federal taxes in the UAE as of yet, but each of the emirates may impose their own taxes. At this time, the Abu Dhabi government contributes the largest portion of tax revenue to the country, at nearly 80 per cent. Dubai contributes another 9 per cent or so and the other emirates combined make up the remainder. Abu Dhabi, Dubai, and Sharjah tax oil and banking businesses, while other small businesses and individuals are still free from paying taxes. Taxes will very likely be forthcoming for them.

BRIBES

On the surface, everything appears to be free, but in reality, a price is being paid. While there may not be Value-Added or Goods and Services Tax or other taxes being imposed, there are bribes. Contractors who bid for jobs may be beaten by another company willing to bid extremely low and pay a kickback. It is an acceptable practice to take a bribe, but not for everyone to know about it. The trend is slowly moving away from this practice because when revealed, it results in scandal.

> The combination of steep competition and behind-the-scenes bribes result in higher costs and corners needing to be cut. These may include the quality of supplies and labour, resulting in shoddy workmanship. This practice has benefited no one but the repair and maintenance industries.

The government, which wields control over the economy, has been so badly burned in some of these deals that it is now implementing laws to force fair business practices.

BUSINESS LICENCES

Some licenses can only be obtained by nationals. Others can be obtained by foreigners who have a national for a partner or sponsor. The national is entitled to between 25 per cent and 51 per cent of the business, depending on the type of license and the location of the business. Business agreements with UAE nationals tend to favour the nationals. There is a free zone called the Jebel Ali Free Zone, located between Dubai and Abu Dhabi, that was established to circumvent the requirement for national participation in foreign enterprise. Jebel Ali has a large port for goods to be shipped in and out. Special licenses, free of any national participation, can be obtained in this zone. However, if business is to be conducted within the country, a national must be hired.

ENVIRONMENTAL ISSUES

The UAE is paying attention to environmental issues. Abu Dhabi is conducting a federal study on the feasibility of nuclear power, and will seek permission from the international community to build a plant in the next decade. With less than a century of oil reserves left, the UAE is creating tax-free investment havens to foster research and development toward a non-petroleum economy.

The government is pushing for greener cooling technology. Air-conditioning accounts for the bulk of power consumed in the UAE, especially during the summer. Villas could certainly make use of the traditional methods but rather than looking to traditional methods, experts are being sought who can help the country minimise its escalating carbon footprint. The UAE consumes more energy per capita giving it the largest carbon footprint in the world.

Dubai has turned to Japan for expertise. Since the 1970 oil crisis, Japan has invested heavily in energy-saving projects and boasts energy consumption that is 70 per cent less than the global average. The expertise of Japanese scientists has been enlisted to build a "cool city" that uses 60 per cent less energy than developments of a similar size. Abu Dhabi is beginning the construction of Masdar City to house 50,000 people in a car-free environment, where people will be moved in automated pods. The city will be entirely solar powered by a 100-megawatt solar plant that will eventually be boosted to 500 megawatts.

For quite a while during the 1970s to 1990s, the countryside was taking on an increasingly disgusting garbage dump appearance. Picnics were unpleasant activities as a result, to say the least. The government is encouraging better environmental practices and the UAE now participates in the Clean Up Arabia effort, where volunteers take part in cleaning up the country and other activities during the environmental awareness "season".

Finally, the UAE is one of the top five water consumers in the entire world. They are amidst a five-year plan to reduce water consumption from as much as 500 litres per person per day down to 350 litres per person per day. The plan includes education and awareness to encourage people to switch off their taps; better management of the resource through water reuse; raising the cost of water to discourage misuse and imposing hefty fines if that does not work. The agriculture and forestry sectors use the bulk of available water and are areas where the greatest reforms need to be made, particularly through water and sewage reuse.

LAW AND THE COURT SYSTEM

In the UAE legal principles, courts and judicial structures are evolving and changing to meet the needs of the people, and it is thus imperative for businesses and individuals to be familiar and updated on the law and the court system, so as not to run foul of it.

Running an efficient and transparent court system is critical both to the UAE and to world governments to create an economically feasible place for its citizens and foreigners to do business, to stimulate growth and to increase economic capital. Transparency also assists the government in operateing more effectively by openly publishing administrative happenings and standards of practice and procedure.

Background

The UAE established itself on 2 December 1971 as a federation. This federation established a system of government, which includes the constitutional right for the seven emirates to join the federal judicial system or to maintain their own independent judicial system within the confines of their respective emirate. Dubai and Ras Al Khaimah opted to maintain their own judicial system and did not join the federal judicial system.

Abu Dhabi, Ajman, Fujairah, Sharjah and Umm Al Quwain organisationally all operate their courts very similarly to the federal and state court systems within the US. The seven emirates have organised the court system into three levels of litigation: Courts of First Instance which are commonly known to Westerners as Trial Courts, Court of Appeal and Federal Supreme Court which is equal to the US Supreme Court; and four different kinds of courts: civil courts, Shari'a courts, criminal courts and special courts.

UAE law is based on Islamic law, otherwise known as Shari'a law. Essentially, the court system is a dual-based system consisting of Shari'a and civil courts. Within the UAE, each emirate administers its own Shari'a court but remains under the jurisdiction of the Federal Supreme Court, excluding Dubai and Ras Al Khaimah. These two emirates have their own Shari'a Council which governs their Shari'a courts.

> Shari'a law comes directly from the Qur'an. Shari'a represents God's plan for the proper order of society for Muslim way of life. Islamic law is without boundaries or country borders, and applies to Muslims wherever they live.

This mixture of Shari'a and the federal court structures can create confusion organisationally. The reasoning behind the confusion is that the Shari'a courts overlap jurisdictionally with the federal court system. Shari'a courts and the federal court system roles have not been completely defined. It is very challenging for Westerners to grasp the idea that religion and government go hand in hand. Shari'a law does not distinguish between Church and State, or the separation of powers.

History Of The Shari'a Court System

Prior to the establishment of Islam, tribes in the region worshiped idols. Tribes would have disputes within their own tribe and outside of their tribe with other people inhabiting the Arabian Peninsula. Each tribe governed itself and dealt with its own social order by way of presenting the issues to the tribal leader. The tribal leader would be the ultimate decider and settler of the dispute. Once Mohammed introduced a new religion to the people of the Arabian Peninsula, Islam became law around the year 900. Islamic law is based on the will of God, and the standards for social order are laid out in the Qur'an. Although the Qur'an does not provide a codified rule of order, it does provide guidance for the people of the UAE. Islamic law scholars and professionals provide assistance and help judges make their decisions on cases presented before them.

Regulatory History Of The Court System

The seven emirates today maintain some autonomy from the federal court system as local authorities can regulate matters within their own emirate. Before the establishment of any court processes and procedures the courts were know as tribunals and prior to 1971, Abu Dhabi formally issued a law which provided standards for regulating the courts of law in both criminal and civil courts. Fujairah followed Abu Dhabi's established court procedure in 1969 and Dubai followed in 1970. Sharjah in 1971 created a civil court to hear commercial, labour and limited criminal hearings. The remaining three emirates established their court processes and procedures in 1971. In 1973 the UAE established its Supreme Court. The most recent law in 1978 established the Courts of First Instance.

Federal Civil Court Structure

The Courts of First Instance are the lowest level court. This court is similar to the US Trial Courts; however, there are notable differences. No juries are involved and the cases are usually heard by a single judge or a panel of judges. A panel of judges maybe selected due to the circumstances of a case. Working papers, motions and proposed orders are submitted (pleadings) to the court and must be in Arabic. The hearings are generally open to the public, but are spoken in Arabic. For the most part the trial proceedings are not published. This court hears cases ranging from commercial matters to transportation law.

The second level is the Federal Appeal Courts. The federal court of appeals will hear appeals from the Court of First Instance.

The highest level of authority is the Federal Supreme Court or the Court of Cassation. This court is located in Abu Dhabi with a president and a certain number of judges not exceeding five in all. The judges are appointed by decree which is issued by the president of the Union after the approval of the Supreme Council. Judges are appointed by term or contract and are only removed if their contract has expired or they die, resign, reach retirement age, sustain permanent illness preventing them from doing their job, or are disciplinarily discharged or appointed to other offices.

Federal Supreme Court Jurisdiction

The Federal Supreme Court has jurisdiction to hear the following matters:

- Disputes between emirates.
- Examination of the constitutionality of Union laws or legislation.
- Interpretation of the Constitution when requested to do so by any Government authority of any emirate.
- Trial of Ministers and senior officials of the government appointed by decree regarding their actions in carrying out their official duties.
- Crimes directly affecting the interest of the emirates.
- Conflict of jurisdiction judicial authority in one emirate and the judicial authority in another emirate.
- Any other jurisdiction questions.

Shari'a Court Structure

All of the seven emirates have a Shari'a Court. The jurisdictional overlap between the civil and Shari'a courts remains undefined. However, it is important to note that non-Muslims can be tried in a Shari'a court and can receive civil and criminal penalties. Shari'a court decisions can be appealed and overturned by the Federal Supreme Court. In most of the emirates this court can hear civil, serious criminal and family matters. Shari'a courts at the federal level have authority to hear appeals tried at the lower level courts regarding serious criminal offenses. Serious criminal offenses can be robbery, rape and murder. The basis of Shari'a court is Islamic law.

Criminal Courts

The criminal court systems mirror that of the UAE's Federal Civil system—Courts of First Instance, Court of Appeal and Federal Supreme Court.

Special Courts

Diwans Court, which means local rulers, is a court which reviews certain types of criminal and civil offences before they go to the prosecutor's office. Additionally, this court will review passed sentences and retain the right to return the cases to the courts of appeal. The Diwans Court often tries cases because they may involve a citizen and a non-citizen. These cases typically involve delays and this prompted the court to review sentencing and other confinement issues.

The UAE also has a Military Court which is very similar to that of Western military court processes and procedures. This court has authority to hear cases that involve military personnel only.

Human Rights And The Practice Of Law

According to the US Department of State, Shari'a law allows for sentences to include flogging of both Muslims and non-Muslims. Flogging has been known to be used in the UAE for punishment of adultery, prostitution, consensual pre-martial sex, for pregnancy outside of marriage, drug and alcohol abuse and defamation of character.

Prison overcrowding is a problem in Dubai and Abu Dhabi. The conditions of the prisons vary widely from emirate to emirate. The US Department of State notes that in 2006 75 per cent of UAE's prison populations were that of non-citizens. There is no formal system of bail. Authorities can temporarily release detainees who deposit money. A passport will be needed or some form of a guarantee signed by a third party to be temporarily released. These rules apply to both citizens and non-citizens.

Defendants who are involved in the loss of life, be it manslaughter or otherwise, can be denied release until payment or compensation to the victim's family has been determined and received. Defendants are only entitled to an attorney once the investigation has been completed by the police department. Defendants are questioned by authorities without an attorney present. There is also no right to a speedy trial. Cases can linger within the system for quite a long time.

Police and prosecutors are required to have a warrant to enter private homes and property. With that said, the US Department of State noted reports of police departments failing to obtain warrants and illegally entering private property. Under UAE's regulations, failing to obtain a search warrant is subject to judicial review and the officers can be held liable for entering and searching without proper documentation.

Family matters for Muslims are dealt with in the Shari'a court. Muslim women are prohibited from marrying non-Muslims and can be arrested and tried in court for doing so. Rape is punishable by death in the UAE as per its Penal Code. However, spousal abuse is not specifically addressed in the Penal code. It is a crime to partake in homosexual activity in all seven emirates.

The UAE allows for freedom of the press without censorship. However, journalists today are still being detained for their published works. This is an area where the government of the UAE is working for change and reform. It is a crime in the UAE to use the Internet in any way that will violate political, social and religious norms. In addition, it is a crime to use the Internet to oppose Islam, to attempt to convert one to a religion other than Islam, insult their religion or to motivate another person to commit sin.

The Price Of Protest
The UAE's Constitution allows for the right to peacefully assemble. However, as recently as November 2007 in Dubai, 25 Emirati teachers protested (peacefully assembled) to demonstrate the unfair labour practice that forces them to leave their teaching jobs and move to other non-related jobs. After their assembly, the teachers were suspended from teaching.

In 2005 Abu Dhabi police promulgated a widespread problem where government officials at the administrative level were involved with nepotism, embezzlement and abuse of power within the agency. After the report the Penal Code was modified, and it is now crime for government officials to abuse their power.

Westerners who commit crimes often serve their sentence and are usually deported. The Emiratis usually turn a blind eye and a deaf ear to expatriates' activities. They do not wish to stir up political strife on the one hand, but on the other they firmly believe in tolerance of other people's beliefs. Still, there are no guarantees and you need to be aware that you do not have the same rights in this country as you may have in your home country. Most criminal proceedings for Westerners are crimes that involve alcohol. Punishments encompass lashings, prison terms, fines or a combination of these.

The US Department of State annually reports that the UAE government generally respects its citizens' rights, but has a poor track record in some areas. For instance, the people do not have power to change their government, and the government restricts freedom of speech and of the press. Working conditions and abuse of foreign domestic servants are serious problems in an economy in which 98 per cent of the private sector workforce is foreign.

Notable Notes Concerning Business Law

According to Shari'a business transaction law, a Westerner should keep two points in mind when doing business in the UAE. Firstly, the charging of interest is strictly prohibited. Money is not something that can be bought or sold, and cannot be traded. Thus, interest earned is not equitable or fair.

In addition, all business risks and rewards are shared at a proportional rate. This rate is based on the initial amount the investor originally assumed.

Although these two items are based on Shari'a law and are not uniformly codified, they are still highly important and much different from that of Western business law.

Chambers Of Commerce

Each emirate has its own customs and laws for doing business. Some of these laws contradict each other. Check with your embassy or the local chamber of commerce for guidance on doing business in your emirate. Do not assume the way you managed your affairs in Dubai will work 20 minutes away in Sharjah. Each emirate has a chamber of commerce which organises the business of the community, such as awarding business licenses and settling inter-emirate business disputes. In the past, this business and the business of the rulers of each of the seven emirates were one and the same.

In the West, chambers of commerce tend to serve and inform the public or to advocate on behalf of individuals and small businesses. This is the ideal, as it serves common people rather than those in power. The chambers of commerce in the UAE are slowly moving towards this ideal, with a federal Economy and Commerce Ministry taking over the issuing of licenses and arbitrating disputes. Some changes are slow to take place in the UAE, particularly those affecting the power of the rulers. While less political involvement is the goal, in reality, the chambers still largely serve the interests of the rulers.

NON GOVERNMENT ORGANISATIONS

'Take of their riches a donation to purify them and to cleanse them thereby...'
–At-Tawubah: 103

The third pillar of Islam is *Zakat* or "purification", the giving of alms, or dues for the poor which while decreasing one's money, provides a person with blessings and growth.

Zakat is paid on different categories of property—gold, silver, money, livestock, agricultural produce and business commodities—and is payable each year after one year's possession at 2.5 per cent of an individual's wealth and assets.

Some people know only to hoard wealth and to add to it by lending it out on interest. Islam's teachings are the very antithesis of this attitude. Islam encourages the sharing of wealth with others and helps people to stand on their own and become productive members of the society.

It is spent on the poor and the needy. Charity is not just recommended by Islam, it is required of every financially stable Muslim. In embracing this belief, the UAE has made great contributions in support of charity and humanitarian works at local, regional and international levels including sending US$ 100 million to the US in support of the devastation caused by Hurricane Katrina in 2005. The UAE has many non-profit organisations established by its rulers. Some of these are Emirates Wildlife Society, Emirates Environmental Group, Emirates World Heart and Dubai Cares. The largest of these is the UAE Red Crescent (RCS) which operates within the country, and also provides major international relief. It provides services to needy families, and establishes orphanages, clinics, special schools and homes for the elderly to the tune of about half a billion US dollars each year. Almost every non-profit with an international focus has a presence in the UAE.

Controversy

Following the 11 September 2001 attack on the World Trade Centres in New York, all non-profits found themselves the focus of attention from the US government, the media and the public at large, in particular the Muslim and Arab NGO sector. There was speculation that funding through the Muslim and Arab NGO sector had occurred through charitable contributions that were then redirected through recipients to terrorist organisations, primarily to Hamas (Hamas is the Arabic acronym for the Islamic Resistance Movement, a Palestinian organisation committed to eliminating Israel and replacing it with an Islamic state). Hamas is considered a terrorist organisation by the US and the West for its

The Emirates Volunteers Association was formed in 1996 to educate people, especially youth, train volunteers, and to try to involve the public in voluntary work that can contribute to the development of society and the country.

suicide attacks on Israel, and is popular among Palestinians for its network of schools, clinics and civic services, as well as its armed resistance to Israeli military occupation. Palestine has roughly a 22 per cent unemployment rate, and many Palestinians are dependent on international charity to survive. The US government is working to expose Hamas for using the posture of charity to hide its militaristic activity and destroy its reputation. The UAE NGOs are striving to operate successful, professional, open and transparent charities.

Voluntary Work

The Emiratis believe volunteerism enhances social solidarity and social development. The government promotes volunteer work and humanitarian organisations, and implements legislation regulating their services to the public. Volunteers throughout the UAE help with telethons, tree-planting, visiting the elderly and sick, and assisting special-need families. The wives of the rulers are often at the forefront of these efforts, calling for the public to get involved with their time and their donations. There is no end to volunteer opportunities. Just identify the type of volunteer work you wish to do, make a list of charities that fit your passion and then research their presence near you.

FINAL ADVICE

Are you able to cope with a new culture, a new job and an entirely new social life all at the same time? Are you willing to? Is your family? To assist you and your family, learn as much as you can about the local customs. Know the standard of education your children will be receiving and know too that the high quality of education your children received back home may not be available in the UAE and if it is, it is probably extremely expensive. Consider the current cost of living and compare it to your own at home. Learn as much as you can about your employer, how long he has been in business, how lucrative his business is or who is funding the business. If a Sheikh is funding it, it will be around as long as the Sheikh wishes it to be and not longer. Find out also about your work conditions and your responsibilities before you go.

FAST FACTS

CHAPTER 10

Lies are the plague of speech.
Bias is the plague of the opinion.
Forgetting is the plague of knowledge.
—Arabic proverb

Official Name
United Arab Emirates (UAE)

Capital City
Abu Dhabi

Flag
Three equal horizontal bands of green, white, and black from top to bottom. There is also a wider vertical red band on the hoist side

National Anthem
Ishy Bilady (Long Live My Nation)
This anthem was created in 1996, and replaced the former anthem that contained no words. The anthem's lyrics and music were decided through a competition won by Aref Al Sheikh Abdullah Al Hassan. The words are:

Live my country, the unity of our Emirates lives
You have lived for a nation
Whose religion is Islam and guide is the Qu'ran
I made you stronger in God's name, oh homeland
My country, my country,
My country, my country
God has protected you from the evils of the time
We have sworn to build and work

Work sincerely, work sincerely
As long as we live, we'll be sincere, sincere
The safety has lasted and the flag has lived,
Oh our Emirates
The symbol of Arabism
We all sacrifice for you, we supply you with our blood
We sacrifice for you with our souls of homeland

Time
Greenwich Mean Time plus 4 hours (GMT + 0400). The time does not change during the summer. This means that there is a three-hour difference between UK and UAE local times in summer and a four-hour difference in winter.

Telephone Country Code
971

Land
In the Middle East, bordering the Gulf of Oman and the Persian Gulf, between Oman and Saudi Arabia

Area
total: 82,880 sq km (51,500 sq miles)
land: 82,880 sq km (51,500 sq miles)

Highest Point
Jabal Yibir (1,527 m / 5,010 ft)

Climate
Desert; cooler in eastern mountains. Temperatures range from a low of 10˚C (50˚F) in winter to a high of 48˚C (118 ˚F) in the summer with a winter mean of 24˚C (75˚F) and a summer mean of 41˚C (105˚F).

Natural Resources
Petroleum, natural gas

Population
Approximately 4,104,695 in 2006

Ethnic Groups And Census Data
2005 census: Emirati 20 per cent, other Arab and Iranian 22 per cent, South Asian 50 per cent, other expatriates (including Westerners and East Asians) 8 per cent. Males (2,547,043) represent 67.6 per cent of the total population; Females (1,222,037) represent 32.4 per cent. Balance of 335,615, or 8 per cent, are in the country illegally and not included in the count though they are likely predominantly male and present for work, which would bring the male population percentage closer to 70 per cent.

Religion
Muslim: 96 per cent (Sunni 80 per cent, Shi'a 16 per cent); Christian, Hindu, and others: 4 per cent

Languages
Arabic is the official language. English is widely spoken, as are Urdu and Hindi. Almost all signs are in both Arabic and English.

Government Structure
Constitutional Republic. A federation with specified powers delegated to the UAE federal government and other powers reserved to member emirates

Administrative Divisions
Seven emirates:
Abu Zaby (Abu Dhabi), Ajman, Al Fujayrah, Ash Shariqah (Sharjah), Dubayy (Dubai), Ra's al Khaymah, Umm al Qaywayn

Currency
Emirati *dirham* (AED, local abbreviation dhs)

Gross Domestic Product (GDP)
US$ 190.2 billion (2007) with real GDP growth continuing at approximately 7 per cent each year

Non-Oil Sectors
Agriculture, poultry, eggs, dairy products, fishing, mining and quarrying, manufacturing, electricity, gas and water; construction, wholesale, retail and maintenance, restaurants and hotels, transportation, storage and communications, real estate and business services, financial enterprises

Airports
The UAE has 35 airports, of which six are international. The main international airport is in Abu Dhabi.

Rulers
It is useful to memorise the tribe or family name of the ruling family of each emirate.

Ruling family of Abu Dhabi: Al Nahyan

Ruling family of Dubai: Al Maktoum

Ruling family of Sharjah: Al Qassimi

Ruling family of Ajman: Al Nuaimi

Ruling family of Umm Al Quwain: Al Moalla

Ruling family of Ras Al Khaimah: Al Qassimi

Ruling family of Fujairah: Al Sharqi

Ruling family of Al-Ain: Al Nahyan

ACRONYMS

People in the United Arab Emirates (UAE) love acronyms.
New ones are made up every day. Here are a few:

AADC	Al-Ain Distribution Company
ADAC	Abu Dhabi Airport Company
ADACH	Abu Dhabi Authority for Culture and Heritage
ADBW	Abu Dhabi Businesswomen Group
ADCB	Abu Dhabi Commercial Bank
ADCCI	Abu Dhabi Chamber of Commerce and Industry
ADCO	Abu Dhabi Company for Onshore Oil Operations
ADDC	Abu Dhabi Distribution Company
ADDF	Abu Dhabi Duty Free
ADEC	Abu Dhabi Education Council
ADFD	Abu Dhabi Fund for Development
ADFEC	Abu Dhabi Future Energy Company
ADHC	Abu Dhabi Holding Company
ADI	Abu Dhabi International Medical Services
ADIA	Abu Dhabi Investment Authority
ADIAS	Abu Dhabi Islands Archaeological Survey
ADMA	Abu Dhabi Marine Areas
ADNEC	Abu Dhabi National Exhibition Company
ADNH	Abu Dhabi National Hotels
ADNOC	Abu Dhabi National Oil Company
ADPC	Abu Dhabi Petroleum Company
ADPC	Abu Dhabi Ports Company
ADSB	Abu Dhabi Ship Building Company
ADSC	Abu Dhabi Sports Club
ADSM	Abu Dhabi Securities Market
ADSSC	Abu Dhabi Sewage Service Company
ADTA	Abu Dhabi Tourism Authority
ADU	Abu Dhabi University
ADWEA	Abu Dhabi Water and Electricity Authority
AGFUND	Arab Gulf Fund for the United Nations
AMF	Arab Monetary Fund
ARN	Arabian Radio Network

ATM	Arabian Travel Market
b/d	Barrels of oil per day
BST	Bulk supply tariff
CEDAW	Convention on the Elimination of All Forms of Discrimination Against Women
CERT	Centre of Excellence for Applied Research and Training
CSICH	Convention for the Safeguarding of Intangible Cultural Heritage
DBTRS	Department of Blood Transfusion and Research Services
DBWC	Dubai Business Women Council
DCA	Dubai Civil Aviation Authority
DDE	Dubai Diamond Exchange
DED	Dubai Department of Economic Development
DEWA	Dubai Electricity & Water Authority
DF	Dubai Financial
DFM	Dubai Financial Market
DGC	Dubai Gems Club
DHCC	Dubai Healthcare City
DIA	Dubai International Airport
DIBS	Dubai International Boat Show
DIC	Dubai International Capital
DIC	Dubai Internet City
DIEC	Dubai International Convention and Exhibition Centre
DKU	Dubai Knowledge Universities
DMCC	Dubai Metals and Commodities Centre
DMI	Dubai Media Inc
DP	Dubai Ports
DPC	Dubai Petroleum Company
DPE	Dubai Petroleum Establishment
DPW	Dubai Ports World
DSF	Dubai Shopping Festival
DSS	Dubai Summer Surprises
DTCM	Dubai Department of Tourism and Commerce Marketing
DTTC	Dubai Tea Trading Centre

Ducab	Dubai Cable Company
DUMA	Dubai Marine Areas
DWTC	Dubai World Trade Centre
EA	Emirates Airline
EAD	Environmental Agency—Abu Dhabi
EBC	Emirates Broadcasting Corporation
EHC	Emirates Heritage Club
EIA	Emirates Identity Authority
EITC	Emirates Integrated Company, referred to as 'du'
EMI	Emirates Media Inc
EMP	Emirates Marketing & Promotions
ENG	Emirates National Grid
ENOC	Emirates National Oil Company
EPC	Emirates Postal Corporation
EPD	Environment Protection Division
EPPCO	Emirates Petroleum Products Company
ESA	Emirates Sailing Academy
EU	Economic Union
FDI	Foreign Direct Investment
FEC	Fujairah Exhibition Centre
FGB	First Gulf Bank
FNC	Ministry of Federal National Council
FoodCo	Abu Dhabi National Foodstuff Company
G2B	Government to Business
G2C	Government to Citizens
G2G	Intra-government
GAD	Guggenheim Abu Dhabi
GAFTA	The Greater Arab Free Trade Area
GCC	Gulf Cooperation Council
GHC	General Holding Corporation wholly-owned by Abu Dhabi
GITEX	Gulf Information Technology Exhibition
GWU	General Women's Union
HCT	Higher Colleges of Technology
HH	His Highness
HMSDC	Harvard Medical School Dubai Center's Institute for Postgraduate Education and Research

HTL	Horizon Terminals Limited of Dubai
IATF	International Autumn Trade Fair, Dubai
ICAD	Industrial City of Abu Dhabi
IDB	Islamic Development Bank
IDEX	International Defense Exhibition & Conference
IJAF	International Jewellery & Accessories Fair
IPIC	International Petroleum Investment Company
IWPP	Independent water and power production plant
JAFZA	Jebel Ali Free Zone
JDA	Joint Development Agreement
Jodco	Japan Oil Development Company
KCT	Khor Fakkan Container Terminal
KEFCO	Kemira Emirates Fertiliser Company
KV	Knowledge Village
MEW	Ministry of Environment and Water
MFN	Most favoured nations
MOE	Ministry of Economy
MOH	Ministry of Health
MOL	Ministry of Labour
NACP	National AIDS Control & Prevention Programme
NDLS	National Disaster Life Support, a training programme
OCAM	Office of Complementary and Alternative Medicine
OPEC	Organisation of the Petroleum Exporting Countries
PTD	Abu Dhabi Public Transport Department
RAK	Ras Al Khaimah
RCS	UAE Red Crescent
RERA	Real Estate Regulatory Authority
RTA	Roads & Transport Authority
SCTDA	Sharjah Commerce & Tourism Development Authority
SEWA	Sharjah Electricity and Water Authority
SIA	Sharjah International Airport

SKMC	Sheikh Khalifa Medical City
SPTC	Sharjah Public Transport Corporation
TDIC	Tourism Development & Investment Company, Abu Dhabi
TECOM	Dubai Technology & Commerce and Free Zone Authority
TRA	Telecommunications Regulatory Authority
UAEU	UAE University
UAQ	Umm Al Quwain
UOG	UAE Offsets Group
UWEC	Union Electricity Water Company (Fujairah)
WAM	Emirates News Agency (Wakalat Anba'a al-Emarat)
ZU	Zayed University

CULTURE QUIZ

Now that you have read the book, try these quiz questions to test your knowledge on how best to react in certain situations. Life in the UAE can be a rewarding experience for those willing to take the time and effort to understand the country and their culture. The best advice to anyone confronted with a new culture is to conduct yourself with respect and courtesy. Your mistakes and indiscretions will usually be overlooked until you have become more comfortable with your new environment.

SITUATION 1

You are a woman and your Emirati employer has invited you to a lavish feast at a five-star hotel. You arrive to find lots to drink, discreet waiters and only two other women. One is a Westerner enjoying herself immensely, the other is a scantily clad Russian dancer putting on a show for five leering men. What do you do?

Ⓐ Relax and enjoy yourself. Your employer is simply letting his hair down, showing you he can accept and enjoy your ways too.

Ⓑ Politely greet everyone and ask to speak to your employer in private. Let your employer know that you did not realise the nature of his invitation and that you do not feel comfortable participating.

Ⓒ Join the festivities but find an excuse to leave soon, such as becoming suddenly ill.

Comments

You may opt for any of the above and everyone decides differently for themselves. The problem with **Ⓐ** is that your employer is flouting his own traditions and beliefs. His behaviour is not acceptable or legal but some Emiratis believe God cannot see them when they are not on holy ground. A Western hotel is certainly not seen as holy ground. While he may enjoy your 'ways', he does not accept them or respect you for them.

Answer **C** will solve your problem in the situation but you will be invited to such occasions again and again. Eventually, you are going to need to go with option **B**. You will begin to recognise these invitations when they are initially made so you can avoid them before you are faced with them. If you opt to participate in them, your reputation will suffer.

There is little that is not known by everyone in such a small place and it becomes difficult to know whom to trust when everyone is talking behind your back. Also, you must think about what kind of a relationship you want with your employer. The more professional it is, the less trouble and conflict you will have. If your employer is inviting you to an occasion involving the women of his family, you are very fortunate and should take advantage of such a privilege without having to fear for your reputation.

SITUATION 2

Upon returning from an extended vacation, you run into one of your well-educated Emirati friends. She informs you she married while you were gone. You express delight and ask her whom she has married. "You mean his name, miss?" she enquires with some dubiousness as to how you could possibly expect to know him. "No," you say, "I mean is he your cousin?" "No!" she exclaims knowing full well cousin marriage is unacceptable in a modern society, "He is my mother's sister's son," she explains. What do you say?

A Explain the blood relationship is the same on the mother's side as it is on the father's.

B Congratulate her and wish her well.

C Express an interest in this new event in her life, question her about how she likes being married, what her new husband is like and how life is different for her now.

Comments

Ⓐ will bring an end to your friendship. Emirati's have different words to express the relationships of paternal and maternal relatives. It is not surprising your friend did not connect the close blood relationship as being the same on her mother's side of the family. At any rate, the deed is done, not only is she powerless to stop or change it, she has probably fallen in love with her husband. It would probably cause her shame to appear as the uneducated desert dweller in front of you.

Ⓑ is your only option. You probably shouldn't have inquired as to her connection with her husband anyway.

Ⓒ is socially unacceptable. You may question a woman endlessly about her siblings, parents and children, but her relationship with her husband is a taboo subject. While a group of Emirati women in a *majlis* setting might talk quite candidly about marital relations and joke endlessly about them, the discussion is always general and never mentions specific examples. Women needing to discuss their personal relationships do so in private with a sister or their mother.

SITUATION 3

You, a Western woman, invite a young Emirati woman to your home for a visit. She arrives accompanied by her older brother and her mother. The brother leaves after handing you a container of hot food and the mother sweeps grandly into your sitting room. Ignoring your sofa and lounge chairs, she settles herself on the floor and pours coffee from her very own thermos for the three of you into the coffee cups she brought along. The mother nibbles at one of the dishes you prepared, but clearly does not like it. She does not speak English and you quickly exhaust your meagre Arabic. Your apartment is hot and the mother soon doses off in an upright position. Circle the things you would do:

Ⓐ Turn up the air-conditioning.
Ⓑ Bring a bowl of water for washing.
Ⓒ Smile, ask your guests if they are comfortable.

D Try to get the mother to sit in a chair.

E Drink their coffee and eat the food they brought.

F Find some floor cushions for everyone to sit on.

G Encourage the mother to use your larger coffee mugs to drink out of.

H Eat the food you prepared and visit with the daughter while you wait for the mother to wake up.

I Turn on some music to fill the silence.

J See them to the door at the end of the visit.

Comments

The only responses that would be inappropriate are **D**, **G**, **I**, and **J**. In this situation it appears that the mother is ascertaining your suitability as a friend for her daughter. You want to make her as comfortable as possible and she is most comfortable on the floor. Planning ahead and already having cushions on the floor as an option would be a brilliant stroke on your part. The mother has brought her own cups because given your different beliefs, it is possible your cups at one time contained alcohol and will never quite be clean again. The mother is probably extremely traditional and any music you possess would be offensive to her. Don't worry, she is comfortable with the silence. Ask after their comfort many times. Use the daughter as a translator to find out more about the mother. The right line of questioning might just bring out some fascinating stories. When they are ready to leave, be sure to walk them all the way to their car. Stand at the curb and wave goodbye until they are well on their way.

SITUATION 4

It is Ramadan and you are sitting on an empty beach with a friend eating lunch. An Arab man comes, sits down and begins chatting with you, "Assalam 'alaykum – How are you?" What do you do?

A Say, "Wa 'alaykum assalam – We are fine thank you, and you?" Offer the man some food.

B Say, "Wa 'alaykum assalam – We are fine al-hamdulilah." Put the food away in the icebox (cooler, chillibin).

☉ Say, "Excuse me, we must go." Pack up your belongings and move to another beach.

Comments

🅐 is an entirely inappropriate response. During Ramadan Muslims are in a heightened spiritual state. It is extremely rude to tempt the man with food and further, it is illegal for you to be caught eating in public in daylight hours during the month of Ramadan.

🅑 is not a bad response especially if it is followed by **☉** soon after. You should try to get the food in the icebox before the man comes close enough to see it. You are probably inappropriately dressed given the time of year and may be regarded as tempting the Arab's thoughts. Such behaviour is more the fault of the tempters than the tempted in this society.

While it is a good idea to move on, **☉** by itself is a little abrupt. Also, you may not have any more privacy on another beach. Foreigners curtail their activities during the month of Ramadan or at least make an increased effort to keep them indoors.

SITUATION 5

You, a woman, climb into a taxi, state your destination and sit back for the ride. The driver pulls into traffic, turns and smiles at you and begins behaving in a suggestive manner. What do you do?

🅐 Yell at him to stop the car. If need be, open your door slightly to indicate you are serious and jump out the instant he brings the car to a stop.

🅑 Ignore him.

☉ Order him to stop the car, pay him and get out.

Comments

🅐 is the only choice. Yelling or speaking to him in a very clear, direct and authoritative manner will intimidate him and show him you are in charge. He will probably stop his behaviour out of fear of being reported to the police. Taxi drivers are very opposed to having a car door open while the car is in motion, it is a very effective way to bring the car to a stop and in traffic you probably aren't going fast enough for this to be dangerous.

B may indicate to him your boundaries are flexible and he should test them further.

C is awfully generous of you but why do you feel you owe him a thing?

SITUATION 6

You, a man, and two female friends have just arrived at what you think is a great campsite. A villager sees you from afar and comes over to warn you of the danger of falling rocks on your campsite. You thank him and chat with him a bit. He wants to know the relationship of you and your two friends. You:

A Explain that you are all just friends out having a nice time. You view this as a good opportunity to educate him in your ways.

B Tell him it is a personal matter you do not wish to discuss.

C State that one of the women is your wife and the other is your sister.

Comments

A will not work. The villager, raised very traditionally, cannot understand this situation any better than you can understand the situation with his women. He probably has not had much contact with foreigners or read a book like this one. You are more likely to shock him than you are to educate him.

B leaves him to form his own impressions, either that you've hired the women or that you are all related. He understands what a private matter women are and may leave the topic alone. However, he sees you as an outsider and therefore not subject to his cultural rules. He may press you further.

If he does, go on to answer **C** if you aren't already there. It is a white lie, but it is also something he can understand because sisters are a part of a man's incest group (people he can't marry) and a wife belongs to him. It is acceptable for you to be in their company.

SITUATION 7

You are driving by yourself on a highway between two cities. Two young Emirati men wearing dishdashas and driving a four-wheel-drive vehicle pull up beside you. They keep abreast of you and try to get your attention. What do you do?

A Ignore them and slow your speed.
B Make rude hand gestures at them.
C Increase your speed in an effort to get away from them.

Comments

A is most likely to get them to leave you alone. Few people here like to drive slowly so the men will grow bored with their game and move on. **B** gives them attention, but could anger them and cause them to do something dangerous like run you off the road.

C is what they are hoping you will do—join in a game of chase. They would really like you to eventually pull over and chat with them, the catch part of the game. You can't outrun them and you might get a ticket trying. Go back to **A**.

SITUATION 8

A male Emirati colleague gives you, a Western woman, an expensive gift of gold jewellery. You remember that to refuse a gift in this culture is rude. You:

A Thank him profusely but refuse the gift explaining that such a gift carries too much meaning in your culture.
B Thank him, accept the gift and treat it lightly.
C Thank him profusely and eagerly accept the gift.

Comments

To refuse a gift is rude. However, if the Emirati man has spent much time in a Western culture, he knows accepting his gift means accepting him too. Gauge his experience and sensitivity to Westerners; if it is high, go with ❶. If his Western experience or sensitivity is less than proficient, go with ❷ and proceed with caution. You might want to have less contact with the man until you are sure of his intentions and he understands yours. ❸ suggests you are open to personal relations and that you may be willing to be intimate if enough presents are extended.

SITUATION 9

You are a Western man sitting by yourself at a corner table of Hardees. You are minding your own business when a black-cloaked woman leaves her group of female friends and approaches your table. She is lightly veiled and her face is uncovered. You can see she is exceptionally beautiful. She says hello, hands you a piece of paper with her name and telephone number written on it, and says, "You will call me?" You:

❶ Apologise, tell her you can't do that, pack up your food and escape.
❷ Thank her, accept the piece of paper, extricate yourself from the situation as soon as politeness will allow and later throw the number away.
❸ Thank her, accept the number, chat with her a bit and call her later, maybe even setting up a time and place to meet.

Comments

❶ is rude and might cause the woman embarrassment in front of her friends, though her behaviour is inappropriate to begin with and would cause her shame if more people knew about it. ❷ is the safest reaction since you allow her to save face. You will want to make the quickest exit possible because of the inappropriate nature of the situation. ❸ is a really bad idea. The whole thing may be a set up and who is going to prevent you from disappearing?

SITUATION 10

You are vacationing or a new resident in the United Arab Emirates and are invited to join a group of people to go shopping and to the beach. You are a woman who wears Western style clothing. This clothing includes very short shorts and a tank top. You wonder if your attire would be appropriate at the shopping centre and the beach as it is very hot outside and you would like to be comfortable and cool. You:

Ⓐ Decide to wear your traditional style western clothing.
Ⓑ Decide to wear pants with your tank top.
Ⓒ Put on a skirt with a shirt with a high neckline that covers most of your arms.

Comments
Ⓐ is for the most part completely unacceptable. You will find westerners and other people who wear shorts and sleeveless shirts; however these are mainly in the urban areas of Dubai and still could be offensive to some people. **Ⓑ** again, might be acceptable in the urban areas but certainly not recommended attire as it is not suggested that women wear pants. **Ⓒ** is your best option. Despite the heat women should dress in a simplistic manner. A high neck-lined shirt with sleeves that cover past the elbows with a skirt that reaches beyond the knees is a good, simple look.

SITUATION 11
You have been invited to speak with a group of Emirati people that includes men and women. Over the time you have spent with them you have developed a friendly and open atmosphere. Everyone has enjoyed your company and your talk. As you are saying goodbye, you:

Ⓐ Shake everyone's hand and let him or her know you had a wonderful time.
Ⓑ You wait for the person to initiate a hand shake.
Ⓒ Point across the room to a person who you would like to say goodbye to and walk up and reach out to them with your left hand as they are on your left.

Comments

There are several types of ways to say goodbye that include good wishes. If you chose **Ⓐ** to shake everyone's hand you might be offending an Emirati male who will not shake hands with a woman, nor do they think it appropriate for you to do so. **Ⓑ** is your best option in this scenario as it is best to wait to see how the other person wants to say goodbye to you. Usually men shake hands with other men and some men will shake hands with a woman but this is not customary. **Ⓒ** is the worst option possible in this situation. Pointing is offensive and your left hand could be considered unclean. A person should always motion and eat with their right hand.

SITUATION 12

Your place of business will be sending you on a business trip to the United Arab Emirates and you have been charged with setting up meetings with other UAE business people. You have the option of setting meetings any day of the week and you must bring gifts to the meeting attendees. You organise the meeting and you:

Ⓐ Set the meeting on a Wednesday and bring a wrapped basket of world teas as a gift.

Ⓑ Set the meetings on Friday and bring with you a nice bottle of aged Scotch as gifts for the meeting attendees.

Ⓒ Set the meeting on Saturday and during the meeting you interrupt the moments of silence with inquiries of the health of an Emirati's wife and daughter and offer perfume with alcohol in it as a gift.

Comments

Ⓐ is the perfect option in this scenario. Wednesdays are good days for meetings. The gift of world teas would be a nice gesture and a very acceptable gift. The gift will be opened in private and not in the open meeting. Friday is a day of rest in the UAE and therefore **Ⓑ** is not a good choice. Any gift that contains alcohol, pork, knives, personal hygiene items, dog toys or pictures of dogs, and images of nudity including paintings or sculptures are not gifts that would be acceptable in the UAE. ❸ is simply not an option because of the communication style. Communication in the UAE can be slow with moments of silence. These moments of silence could be an indication of a silent observer who might be the decision maker. A person at a meeting who asks questions and speaks frequently could be a person who may not be as important as the person who is the silent observer. Additionally, one should never inquire about an Emirati's wife or daughter. It is best to not discuss women at all with an Emirati business man. It should also be noted that often meetings are interrupted by business calls and visits from family or friends. This is not because the Emirati believes the meeting is unimportant this is simply customary. Further, it is vital to learn the full names of the meeting attendees and how they would like to be addressed.

DO'S AND DON'TS

DO'S
General

- Wear loose modest clothing with elbows, knees and necks covered.
- Do prepare to dress better than you did back home.
- Remember that shaking someone's hand on a deal is as good as signing a contract.
- Make friends with people of the same gender.
- Remember you are a visitor and a guest.
- Respect the local laws, culture and Muslim sensibilities of the UAE.
- Carry a copy of your passport or your driver's license at all times.
- Go to bars with at least one other person if you are a single woman. Too many unaccompanied visits will harm your reputation among even the expatriates.
- Travel with at least one other person whenever possible, particularly when outside the city, at night or if you are a woman.
- Leave the lights on when away from home.
- Lock doors and windows of your residence especially when away from home.
- Have a friend check on your home when you are away for any length of time.
- Lock your car, even when driving.
- Use caution when riding in taxicabs. Sit in the back seat of the cab and avoid interaction with the driver other than destination instructions, especially if you are alone. Use the seat belt if one is available.
- Treat the local population with the same respect you would expect back home.
- Frequent the same stores for your regular shopping. The store owners will begin to know you and feel responsible for you so you will not be hassled or followed by store employees or customers.
- Negotiate price.

- Realise 'yes' may only mean 'possibly' or 'maybe'.
- Compromise in order to save face or avoid shame—both yours and that of the Emiratis.
- Try to acquire *wasta*.
- Speak positively.
- Expect gushy, flowery personal correspondence, as Arabic is an emotional language.
- Shake hands with a person of the same gender as you. Men should allow an Emirati or Arab woman to decide if she will shake hands. Western women should err on the side of caution and not extend a hand to an Emirati man, unless he extends his hand first.
- Stand when people enter a room except if the person is a servant or tea boy.

Entertaining

- Keep pets locked up when entertaining.
- Show photographs of your family. People in photographs should be adequately covered by Emirati standards.
- Be prepared for direct and blunt questions such as, "Are you married?" In return, ask "How are you?".
- Be hospitable, and offer food and drink (except during the Ramadan period).
- Respond with '*insha' allah'* when someone talks about the future.
- If you must, bring a simple gift when visiting an Emirati home such as flowers or candy. However, you are not expected to bring anything at all.
- Expect to be separated from the other gender in social situations.
- Remove your shoes in an Emirati house.
- Expect to be abandoned for 15–30 minutes suddenly when your host goes to pray.
- Eat only with your right hand.
- Accept coffee or tea whenever it is offered.

Business

- Expect a lack of punctuality and be patient.
- Extend special favours or concessions in business dealings

as your relationship with an Emirati deepens.
- Schedule your appointments for the morning if possible.
- Carry business cards with English on one and Arabic on the other side of the card.
- Request full names of Emiratis you will meet or correspond with be written for you in English.

DON'TS
General
- Don't wear a veil or the traditional dress if you are a non-Muslim woman.
- Don't kiss in public.
- Don't criticise the government.
- Don't be lulled into a false sense of security; crime does occur.
- Don't leave valuables unsecured.
- Don't take drugs. They carry a lengthy jail sentence. Those caught bringing them into the country are charged with trafficking and sometimes receive a life sentence.
- Don't possess pornography of any sort. This is illegal.
- Don't drink and drive. The law is zero tolerance and strict penalties apply.
- Don't become argumentative or abusive. It is not permitted; nor is public drunkenness.
- Don't stare at or distract someone who is praying.
- Don't refuse money to a beggar (you will see very few of them in this part of the Arab world). Give a token amount or the blessing *'Allah yateek'*, meaning God give you.'
- Don't make critical remarks about any religious practice.
- Don't shake a man's hand if you are a woman or a woman's hand if you are a man.
- Don't enquire about women.
- Don't discuss Israel, alcohol, drugs or sex.
- Don't criticise or display strong or negative emotion in public.
- Don't discuss your humble origins; you will only embarrass yourself. Don't boast of your achievements either. Fortune and unearned wealth are more greatly admired. Wait for them to ask.

- Don't express dislike of a relative and do not bring up fantastic tales of a black sheep in your family. Family is respected and protected. Dirty laundry is not aired.
- Don't point the soles of your feet at another person.
- Don't point at another person.
- For women, don't wear a bikini on a beach in Sharjah.
- Don't use the 'thumbs up' gesture; it is offensive.
- Don't photograph people without first obtaining their permission. Never photograph Emirati women.
- Don't take photographs of airports, docks, industrial and military sites, government buildings or telecommunications installations.

Entertaining

- Don't admire your hosts' belongings, they may feel obliged to give them to you as a gift.
- Don't open a gift in front of the person who gave it to you.
- Don't serve Emirati guests pork or alcohol. In fact, labelling dishes at a large gathering with a buffet is advisable.

Work

- Don't be offended at interruptions during business meetings.
- Don't conduct business on Friday.

GLOSSARY

DAILY EXPRESSIONS

A little	*Shwaya / Shway*
Alright	*Zen*
Can you help me?	*Mumken tsaa'dni?*
Congratulations	*Mabrook*
Don't mention it	*Afwan*
Goodbye	*Ma'a ssalama*
Good morning	*Sabah alkhayr* (morning of goodness)
Hello / Welcome	*Marhaba*
How are you?	*Keef halak?* (to a man) *Keef halik?* (to a woman)
How much?	*Kam?*
I understand	*ana fahim* (by man) *ana fahma* (by woman)
I don't understand	*ana afhim* (by man) *ana afham* (by woman)
If it be God's will	*Insha'allah*
Impossible	*Mish mumkin*
Maybe / Perhaps	*Mumkin*
My name is...	*Esmi*
Never mind / It doesn't matter	*Ma'alesh*
Peace be upon you	*Assalam 'alaykum*
Peace be upon you too	*Wa 'alaykum assalam*
Thank you	*Shukran*
Thanks be to God	*Al hamdu lilah*
That which is forbidden	*Haram*
That's fine / Perfect	*Tamam*
There is no problem	*Mafi mooshcola*

There is some	*Fi*
There isn't any	*Ma'afi*
This	*Hadha*
Welcoming someone into your home or office	*Ahlan wa sahlan*
What God wills	*Masha'allah*
What is your name?	*Esmak eh?*
What time is it?	*El-saa kam?*
Where can I make a telephone call?	Fein mumken atalfein
Yes	*Na'am / aiwa*
No	*La'a*
I don't speak Arabic	*Ma-batkallamsh 'arabi*
Do you speak English?	*Int betetkalem inglizi?*
I speak English	*Ana batkallem englizi*

FOOD

Breakfast	*Fetar*
Lunch	*Ghada*
Dinner	*Asha*
Water	*Mayya*
Mineral water	*Mayya maadania*
Barbequed	*Mesh-wee*
Chicken	*Da-jaj*
Fish	*Sa-mak*
Meat	*La-han*
Milk	*Haleeb*
Soup	*Shourba*
Spices	*Nashif*
Stew	*Saloona*
Stuffed	*Mah-shee / mashwee*

MEAL TIME EXPRESSIONS

In the name of God (said just prior to eating)	*Bismillah*
By God you should eat (said by host)	*Billah alaich tihbshi*
You did not eat (said by host)	*Ma habashtu*
May God honour you / May God bestow his grace on you (said when you are finished eating)	*Akramch Allah / Allah yin'am 'alaich*
To your health (response from host)	*Bil 'afiah*
May God make you healthy and happy (your response)	*Allah yilafich* (male) *Yhannich* (female)

GETTING AROUND / TRAVEL

How do you say... in Arabic?	*Kef igul... bila'arabi?*
I want an interpreter	*Urid mutarjem*
I want to go to	*Ayez arrouh ella*
Is it far?	*Uhwe bi'ib?*
Is it near?	*Uhwe girib?*
May I sit here?	*Mumkin ag'id hina?*
Please wait for me	*Law samaht intidherni*
Straight	*Seeda*
To the left	*Yasaar*
To the right	*Yameen*
Wait	*Intazir*
What does this mean?	*Shu ya'ani*
When does the....arrive?	*Mata tosal il...?*
When does the...leave?	*Mata yamshi il...?*
Where is...?	*Fein*
Which bus goes to...?	*Ai bas yrouh il...?*

DAYS OF THE WEEK

Monday	*E-etnein*
Tuesday	*El-talat*
Wednesday	*El-arbaa*
Thursday	*El-khamees*
Friday	*El-jumaa*
Saturday	*El-sabt*
Sunday	*El-had*

NUMBERS

Zero	*Sifir*
One / first	*Wahed / awwal*
Two / second	*Etnein / dhani*
Three / third	*Talata / dhalidh*
Four / fourth	*Arbaa / rabi*
Five / fifth	*Khamsa / khamis*
Six	*Sitta*
Seven	*Sabaa*
Eight	*Tamania*
Nine	*Tesaa*
Ten	*Ashaara*
Fifty	*Khamsin*
One hundred	*Mia*
One thousand	*Alf*

RESOURCE GUIDE

USEFUL NUMBERS
Country code
971

Area codes
- Abu Dhabi city   02
- Al-Ain   03
- Ajman, Sharjah and Umm Al Qaiwain   06
- Dubai city   04
- Rywaus and Jebel Dhanna   052
- Fujairah   070
- Ras Al Khaimah   077

Emergency
Abu Dhabi and Fujairah:
- Police   999
- Ambulance   998
- Fire   997

Everywhere else:
- Police / Ambulance / Fire   999

HEALTH
There are over 100 hospitals and clinics available in the UAE as of late 2007. To find one near you, log on to the following websites:
- http://www.hospitalsworldwide.com/hospitals.php?country = UAE
- http://www.global-health-insurance.com/country/uae/hospital.php

Many are open 24 hours a day, seven days a week. Visitors can take up UAE medical insurance or an international plan; many employers provide medical coverage for their employees. Public hospitals do not charge for emergencies and generally have good medical facilities. Few ambulances are equipped with life-saving equipment or manned by trained paramedics and because of severe traffic congestion, they are slow to respond. Request a doctor when calling an ambulance to ensure emergency medical care. Private medical facilities generally do not admit patients who are critically ill or injured because not all medical staff are trained in emergency procedures. The Emiratis themselves tend to fly to major medical facilities in London and elsewhere for their treatment and this expense is covered by the UAE government.

Pre-Entry Vaccinations

Hepatitis B shots are recommended for infants and children 11–12 years of age, or if you have been exposed to blood or sexual contact with locals, or plan to stay longer than six months.

AIDS

AIDS is a taboo topic in the UAE and across the region. Such issues are hidden behind social and religious barriers and are not openly discussed. Foreigners, who account for around 80 per cent of a total UAE population of over four million people, should be HIV-negative as they are subjected to blood tests before being granted residency permits. If a foreigner is found to be infected he or she is immediately deported. The UAE does not report the number of nationals infected with the HIV virus to the World Health Organisation. Care, caution and common sense are prudent tools for maintaining good health everywhere in the world and particularly where barriers exist to hide unpleasant realities.

HIGHER EDUCATION

- Ajman University College of Science and Technology
  Website: http://www.ajman.ac.ae
- American University in Dubai
  Website: http://www.aud.edu
- American University of Sharjah
  Website: http://www.aus.edu
- Emirates Aviation College
  Website: http://www.emiratesaviationcollege.com

- Dubai University College
  Website: http://www.duc.ac.ae
- Etisalat College of Engineering
  Website: http://www.ece.ac.ae
- Higher Colleges of Technology
  Website: http://www.hct.ac.ae
- United Arab Emirates University
  Website: http://www.uaeu.ac.ae
- University of Sharjah
  Website: http://www.sharjah.ac.ae
- Zayed University
  Website: http://www.zu.ac.ae

MAIDS
- Koala Recruitment Centre
  P.O. Box No. 61848 Dubai
  Tel: 266 6061/5771
  Mobile: 050 778 7546
  The company offers international skilled and unskilled housemaids.
- Ready Maids
  P.O. Box 25817 Dubai
  Tel: 0097150 6559371
  Website: http://www.readymaidsuae.com

Look also in the classifieds of the English newspapers, as maids will list their services. However rely mostly on referrals. Many maids live with their employers who provide them with visas. Generally, maids often accept drop-in jobs they can do on their day off to supplement their income.

TRAVEL AGENTS
- DNATA
  P.O. Box No. 1515 Dubai
  Tel: 228 151
  Website: http://www.dnata.com
The website is not user friendly, but it does give a list of all telephone and fax numbers for DNATA offices in the Emirates. Refer to it for matters regarding accommodation

in Dubai, Sharjah, Ras al-Khaimah and Fujairah, travel visas, and cargo shipping.

CAR RENTAL

Visit http://www.dwtc.com. You will need your passport, two photographs and a valid international or a national license.

INSURANCE

- Emirates Insurance Company
  Emirates Insurance Company Building P.O. Box No. 3856
  Abu Dhabi
  Tel: (9712)644 044
  Website: http://www.emirates-ins.com

BUSINESS HOURS

Government offices are open Sunday to Thursday from 7:30 am to 2:30 pm. Private business office hours are 8:00 am to 1:00 pm and 4:00 pm to 8:30 or 9:00 pm. The weekend is now officially Friday and Saturday. Shopping centres open between 8:00 am and 10:00 am, and close between 22:00 pm and midnight.

CREDIT CARDS

Most major credit cards are accepted in the main hotels and larger shops. Carry cash for shopping in the *souks*.

HOTELS

Accommodation in the UAE tend to be of a very high standard. Most of the world's top hotel chains are represented in the major cities. The very finest hotel in the country is the Burj al-Arab in Dubai. Five-star hotels have swimming pools, tennis courts, fully-equipped health centres, fine dining and shopping. The hotels located on the waterfront have excellent beaches with extensive water sports facilities and offerings. Their beach access is generally protected from the public but day visitors can pay a steep fee to use them.

Lesser quality hotel apartments abound. These are an excellent choice if you are staying a week or more and would like to eat some of your meals in as they often come with kitchens. Book these before you arrive in the UAE as the price you get online is far more competitive than what you will be charged in the country.

Some websites you might look for accommodation:

- http://www.dubaitourism.co.ae/hotel
- http://www.uaeregister.org
- http://www.hotels-shopper.com
- http://www.goDubai.com
- http://www.planctholiday.com
- http://www.uae.travelmall.com
- http://www.hotelstravel.com

BANKING

- Arab Bank
  Website: http://www.arabbank.com
- Commercial Bank of Dubai
  Website: http://www.cbd.co.ae
- Emirates Bank International
  Website: http://www.emiratesbank.com
- HSBC Bank Middle East
  Website: http://www.middleeast.hsbc.com
- Middle East Bank
  Website: http://www.ebil.co.ae
- National Bank of Abu Dhabi
  Website: http://www.nbad.co.ae
- National Bank of Dubai
  Website: http://www.nbd.co.ae

ELECTRICITY

Electric voltage used in Abu Dhabi is 240 volts AC and in north Emirates, 220 volts AC. Three-pin outlets are common.

VISAS

All visitors except nationals of Bahrain, Kuwait, Qatar, Oman and Saudi Arabia (the GCC) require a visa. A great many citizens of other nations are automatically given a 60 day visa renewable another 30 days upon their arrival for a maximum stay of 90 days. Since this is provided upon arrival, it is not necessary to obtain in advance. Transit visas are good for

96 hours for those who are not staying. Israeli nationals are not issued visas and those with an Israeli stamp in their passport are not allowed in the country. Visa requirements change periodically so check with your closest UAE embassy for requirements in advance of your trip.

POSTAL SERVICE

Mail takes from five to ten days to reach its international destination. Stamps can be bought from post offices, card shops and even some supermarkets. Place mail in one of the red post boxes located at post offices and shopping centres or your hotel will handle it for you.

CHAMBERS OF COMMERCE

- Abu Dhabi Chamber of Commerce
  POB: 662
  Tel: 02 6214000
  Fax: 02 6215867
  Email: mohd.almehairbi@adcci.gov.ae
  Website: http://www.adcci-uae.com
- Ajman Chamber of Commerce & Industry
  POB: 662 Ajman
  Tel:06 7422177
  Fax: 06 7427591
  E-mail: ajmchmbr@emirates.net.ae
  Website: http://www.ajcci.gov.ae
- Dubai Chamber of Commerce and Industry
  POB: 1457 Dubai
  Tel: 04 2280000 / 2224651
  Fax: 04 2211646
  Email: dcciinfo@dcci.org
  Website: http://web.dcci.ae
- Ra's al-Khaimah Chamber of Commerce and Industry
  POB: 87 Ra's al-Khaimah
  Tel: 07 2333511
  Fax: 07 2330233
  Email: rakchmbr@emirates.net.ae

- Fujairah Chamber of Commerce, Industry & Agriculture
  POB: 738, Fujairah
  Tel: 09 2222400
  Fax: 09 2221464
  Email: fujccia@emirates.net.ae
  Website: www.fcci.gov.ae
- Sharjah Chamber of Commerce and Industry
  POB: 580 Sharjah
  Tel: 06 5682888
  Fax: 06 5681119
  E-mail: scci@sharjah.gov.ae
  Website: www.sharjah.gov.ae
- Umm al-Qaiwain Chamber of Commerce & Industry
  POB: 436 Umm al-Qaiwain
  Tel: 06 7651111
  Fax: 06 7657055
- Ministry of Economy and Commerce
  Website: http://www.uae.gov.ae/Ministries/moec.htm

LEGAL AID AGENCIES

The Legal Resource Guide at http://www.ilrg.com gives country-by-country laws, regulations, referrals and advice. If you get in trouble, contact your embassy.

OTHER USEFUL WEBSITES

- http://www.arabicnews.com
  A good source of news taken from around the Middle East region.
- http://www.dubaicityguide.com
  This website gives you information on the places and services available in Dubai.
- http://www.dubaigolf.com
  You can find information on the luxurious golf courses located in Dubai at this website.
- http://www.uaeinteract.com
  This website brings you the latest news in the UAE.
- http://www.directrooms-uae.com
  Find and book accomodation at hotels and resorts around the UAE here.

- http://www.gulfnews.com
  A UAE-based website that focuses on news taking place in the country and around the region.
- http://www.khaleejtimes.com
  Another UAE-based website.
- http://www.emirates.com
  Plan and book your next flight with the official international airlines of the UAE.
- http://www.etisalat.co.ae
  Visit this website for matters regarding Internet and mobile phone services.
- http://www.uaedesertchallenge.com
  The official website of the UAE Desert Challange, a famous motor sport event.
- http://www.uae-embassy.org
  Website of the UAE Embassy in Washington DC.

FURTHER READING

A Century in Thirty Years: Sheikh Zayed and the United Arab Emirates. Joseph A. Kechichian. Middle East Policy Council, 2000.

A Concise Encyclopedia of Islam. Gordon D. Newby. One World Publications, 2002.

Archaeology of the United Arab Emirates: Proceedings of the First International Conference on the Archaeology of the U.A.E. Hassan Al Naboodah, Daniel T. Potts and Peter Hellyer. Trident Press, 2003.

Doing Business with the United Arab Emirates (Global Market Briefings Series). Phillip Dew. GMB Publishing, 2002.

Folklore and Folk life in the United Arab Emirates (Culture and Civilization in the Middle East). Sayyid Hamid Hurriez. Sayyid H. Hurriez Curzon Press, 2002.

Islam: A Short History. Karen Armstrong. Modern Library, 2005.

Islam Between East and West. Alija Ali Izetbegovic. American Trust Publications, 1993.

Lonely Planet Dubai Encounter. Terry Carter and Lara Dunston. Lonely Planet Publications, 2007.

The Kalevala or Poems of the Kalevala District. F P Magoun. Harvard University Press, 1963, reprinted 1985.

Spectrum Guide to the Untied Arab Emirates. Camerapix. Interlink Books, 2002.

The Architecture of the United Arab Emirates. Salama S. Damluji. Ithaca Press, 2006.

The Emirates—A Natural History. Peter Hellyer and Simon Aspinall. Trident Press, 2005.

The New Book of Middle Eastern Food. Claudia Roden. Knopf, 2000.

The Seven Sheikdoms: Life in the Trucial States before the Federation of the United Arab Emirates. Ronald Codrai. Stacey International, 1990.

The World of Islam. National Geographic Society, 2001.

Time Out Dubai: Abu Dhabi and the UAE. Time Out Guides. Time Out Publications, 2007.

To Be a Muslim, Islam, Peace and Democracy. Prince El Hassan bin Talal. Sussex Academic Press, 2004.

UAE At A Glance. Published in Cooperation with National Media Council, UAE. Trident Press, 2007.

UAE Free Zone Investment Guide. Cross Border Legal Publishing, 2005.

UAE Off-road Explorer. Shelley Frost. Explorer Publishing, 2003.

Understanding Arabs: A Guide for Modern Times. Margaret K. Nydell. Intercultural Press, Boston, Maine, 2005.

Unemployment Evolution in the GCC Economies: Its Nature and Relationship to Output Gaps. Sulayman S. Al-Qudsi. Internet, 2005.

United Arab Emirates. Lisa McCoy. Mason Crest Publishers, 2003.

United Arab Emirates: A New Perspective. Ibrahim Al-Abed and Peter Hellyer. Trident Press, 2001.

United Arab Emirates Business Law Handbook. International Business Publications USA, USA IBP, 2004.

United Arab Emirates Yearbook: 2007 and 2006. Ibrahim Al-Abed, Paula Vine, Peter Hellyer and Peter Vine, Trident Press.

Unveiling Islam: An Insider's Look at Muslim Life and Beliefs. Ergun Mehmet Caner and Emir Fethi Caner. Kregel Publications, 2002.

Women and Globalization in the Arab Middle East: Gender, Economy, and Society. Eleanor Abdella Doumato and Marsha Pripstein Posusney. Lynne Rienner Publishers, 2003.

ABOUT THE AUTHOR

Gina Crocetti Benesh, an American, was born to a military family who frequently moved and often lived in foreign countries. Her early adaptation to other cultures fostered a deep curiosity about other people and perspectives.

She earned her masters degree in Teaching English to Speakers of Other Languages (TESOL) from Portland State University in 1992 and accepted her first teaching position at the United Arab Emirates University in Al Ain. Through the generosity of the Emirati administrators at the UAE University, Mrs. Benesh also earned the widely respected Royal Society of Arts degree in Teaching English as a Foreign Language to Adults (RSA TEFLA) from Cambridge University while teaching full time.

Mrs. Benesh returned to the US in 1999 and transitioned into the non-profit arena in the area of development. She works in the field of philanthropy today. A fan of education, Mrs Benesh continues to study and pursue a variety of interests from marketing to real estate development.

Beautiful to behold during the day or at night, the Burj Al-Arab is a seven-star hotel resembling a billowing sail that dominates Dubai's waterfront.

INDEX

Titles in the CultureShock! series:

Argentina	France	Russia
Australia	Germany	San Francisco
Austria	Hawaii	Saudi Arabia
Bahrain	Hong Kong	Scotland
Beijing	Hungary	Shanghai
Belgium	India	Singapore
Bolivia	Ireland	South Africa
Borneo	Italy	Spain
Brazil	Jakarta	Sri Lanka
Britain	Japan	Sweden
Bulgaria	Korea	Switzerland
Cambodia	Laos	Syria
Canada	London	Taiwan
Chicago	Malaysia	Thailand
Chile	Mauritius	Tokyo
China	Morocco	Turkey
Costa Rica	Munich	United Arab
Cuba	Myanmar	Emirates
Czech Republic	Netherlands	USA
Denmark	New Zealand	Vancouver
Ecuador	Paris	Venezuela
Egypt	Philippines	
Finland	Portugal	

For more information about any of these titles, please contact any of our Marshall Cavendish offices around the world (listed on page ii) or visit our website at:

www.marshallcavendish.com/genref